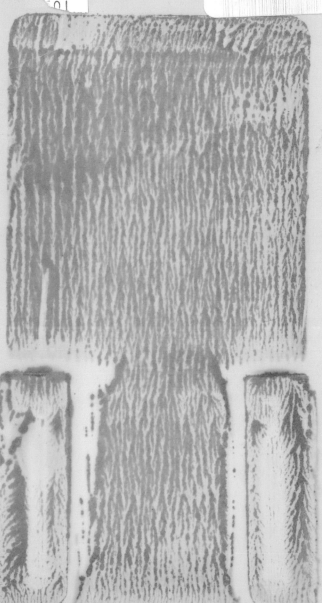

CANDLE IN
THE WIND

CANDLE in the WIND

A Play in Three Acts

By
MAXWELL ANDERSON

ANDERSON HOUSE
Washington, D.C.
1941

NOTE

AMATEUR RIGHTS

GEORGE BANTA PUBLISHING COMPANY, MENASHA, WISCONSIN

By Way of Preface

THOSE who are old enough to remember the nineteen-twenties will recall one curious fallacy of that decade, a belief more extraordinary than the prosperity that accompanied it. The victory over Germany and the efflorescence of invention that went with and followed the war staggered men's minds. They saw the earth and its creatures in a bright new scientific light in which the customs of our ancestors appeared to be based on inexplicable and ridiculous taboos. Religion was not only questioned, but put aside. Social codes were scrutinized under microscopes, and scrapped along with the rules of Leviticus. There was a general belief that men were done with the foolishness of wars and conquest as a method of settling differences. On this side of the Atlantic at least, we thought men had learned better than to try again to grasp the steering wheel of the earth by violence. We closed our eyes to smoking volcanoes of malignity, wondering foolishly how men would adjust themselves to a life in which there was no more hell fire. We believed that the war had been a mistake, that no war was worth fighting, even for the victor; that Gandhi was right, that non-resistance was more powerful than force, that the conqueror destroyed himself automatically, that good and evil came in unavoidable waves, that good would inevitably turn into evil and evil into good with the passage of years. We rejected the war between good and evil. We would fight it no more. Villains were made villains by circumstances, and we must fight the circumstances, not the poor, individual wretches whose anti-social actions caused trouble. Peace conferences were held and humane agreements concerning the usages of war were made among the nations. Naval strength was adjusted by treaty, and battleships were sunk to limit the power of those who had too much. It was an age of reason and good feeling that seemed destined to last interminably. Having emerged into sunlight out of the darkness of history, we saw our way clearly. We saw clearly in those high-minded times that the race was not going to live by the Old or the New Testament. It was going to live in the light of scientific day, making its choices freely among the fruits of the new trees of knowledge. Crime was a disease, and curable. Poverty was a disease, and curable. God was to be replaced by a sort of higher expediency, arrived at by laboratory methods. There was no sin except that which made for inefficiency. Honor was a holdover from the past, retained mainly for business reasons. The need for sexual restraint was abolished by the discovery of contraceptives. Men were like trees, the race was like a forest. They needed nothing except proper conditions and free functioning to grow and prosper as never before. If there had been scarcities, if men had lacked and suffered, all lacks could be supplied by the multiplication of machinery. If there had been grim and terrible feuds over the love of a woman, the ownership of land or the conflicts of worship, these were become laughably unnecessary. Love should be free, land should bear beyond the capacity of the race to consume, religion was a laid ghost. We were to go forward and eat and drink and be merry, and right and wrong would dissolve into a series of realistic choices between that which was healthful and that which was poisonous.

Since every man's thinking is directed or deflected by that of his age we all of us, in the nineteen-twenties, stared hard at this new and dazzling age which we were assured was just beyond the next elections. To most people it was not only acceptable but welcome as an inevitable step forward. What kind of environment it would make for us if it came none of us knew. What dangers lurked under its shiny blessings we could only guess. There was no precedent for the utopia of invention. Men were mainly concerned, then, as always, with the problem of keeping some kind of place for themselves, philosophically and economically, on this whirling ball. It was no longer expected that the gods would help us. We knew no gods and honored no decalogue. We had a low opinion of the race of men and therefore of ourselves.

Yet it was in these godless nineteen-twenties that I stumbled upon the only religion I have. And I came upon it in the most unlikely and supposedly godless of places. I was a journalist, and I knew nothing about the theatre except casually from the outside. But I wrote a verse tragedy, being bored with writing editorials, and a gallant producer put it on the stage—for no reason that I can see now. It failed quietly, as it deserved, but after its production the theatre tugged at me, its rewards dazzled me—and I wrote other plays, some of them successful. However, from the very beginning the theatre was to me, in some fundamental ways, an exasperating puzzle. Some plays succeeded, some did not, and why, nobody knew. Success on the stage seemed to be one of the ultimate mysteries. Leaving aside the questions of acting and directing, the problems of theme, story and writing appeared only more confused when discussed by the professors of playwriting. I developed a theory, which still looks cogent to me, that a playwright's first success was always largely accidental. After that he could analyze what he had done—and begin to develop an intuition that would take him through the maze of difficulties and dangers his action and dialogues must thread. But intuition is an unreliable guide, and I was not as intuitive as some others. I needed a compass—or a pole star—or some theory of what the theatre was about, and I had none.

However, I did discover that there were rules of playwriting which could not be broken. One by one I unearthed them for myself, or dug them out of the treatises of predecessors. And by and by some of them began to look like essentials, because every time I broke them I was rapped over the knuckles by the public. Let me cite a few of the first that came painfully clear to me.

(1) The story of a play must be the story of what happens within the mind or heart of a man or woman. It cannot deal primarily with external events. The external events are only symbolic of what goes on within.

(2) The story of a play must be a conflict—and specifically, a conflict between the forces of good and evil within a single person. The good and evil to be defined, of course, as the audience wants to see them.

(3) The protagonist of a play must represent the forces of good and must win, or, if he has been evil, must yield to the forces of the good, and know himself defeated. It might be possible to write a play in which the hero was evil, and thought himself victorious—but the playwright would have to indicate that he did not agree.

(4) The protagonist of a play cannot be a perfect person. If he were he could not improve, and he must come out at the end of the play a more admirable human being than he went in.

When I had once begun to make discoveries of this sort they came thick and fast. And they applied not, as is natural to suppose, to extraordinary plays only—to Shakespeare and Jonson and the Greeks—but to all plays, and to those in our modern repertory as much as any others. I add a few more of the ancient and inescapable rules as they were beaten into me.

(5) The protagonist of a play must be an exceptional person. He or she cannot be run-of-the-mill. The man in the street simply will not do as the hero of a play. If a man be picked from the street to occupy the center of your stage, he must be so presented as to epitomize

qualities which the audience can admire. Or he must indicate how admirable human qualities can be wasted or perverted—must define an ideal by falling short of it, or become symbolic of a whole class of men who are blocked by circumstances from achieving excellence in their lives.

(6) Excellence on the stage is always moral excellence. A struggle on the part of a hero to better his material circumstances is of no interest in a play unless his character is somehow tried in the fire, and unless he comes out of his trial a better man.

(7) The moral atmosphere of a play must be healthy. An audience will not endure the triumph of evil on the stage.

(8) There are human qualities for which the race has a special liking on the stage. In a man, positive character, strength of conviction not shaken by opposition; in a woman, fidelity, passionate faith. These are qualities which are especially disliked on the stage: in a man, cowardice, any refusal to fight for a belief; in a woman, self-pity, or lack of pity for others, or an inclination toward the Cressid.

These are precepts, of course, only for the writing of a play. The presentation is quite as important, and hedged about with as many commandments, but since I am neither actor nor director I am aware of only a few. Let me indicate what some of them are. When you choose an actor to play the leading role in a play you try to find a man who is not only a good actor, but who can be looked upon with admiration by the people out in front. This may seem simple enough to do, but it is not. When you are casting a play you become acutely conscious of the mental, physical and moral short-comings of the human race. If you will stand in the lobby of a theatre as the patrons come in and examine them with the idea of finding a man or a woman who could take a leading part in the play, you will be disconcerted by the imperfection of mankind. So few, so lamentably few, would stand the test of the center of the stage, the concentrated lights and the concentrated scrutiny of a thousand fellow creatures insistent on perfection, or an approach to perfection. In that pool of light at the center of the stage all defects are magnified. Pick out the handsome, the attractive, the beautiful, the youthfully engaging and let the dissecting stares play on them one by one. Suppose you have chosen the best out of thousands. Suppose they are all attractive at first glance. But look again, for the audience will look again. Perhaps in one you find a too heavy jaw, in another slightly thin nostrils, or an inadequate forehead, a shifty eye, faintly clumsy legs, an awkward pose, over-eagerness, timidity, a slight indication of grossness, illness, hesitant speech. Physical defects are less disastrous than mental or spiritual faults. One in ten thousand will be worthy to stand in that blaze, and like as not that one, even if he be an actor, is a bad one, tied up emotionally, unable to pour his soul into words and emotional states not his own.

I list these technical difficulties because they began eventually to have one meaning for me. They mean that the purpose of the theatre is to find, and hold up to our regard, what is admirable in the human race. The theatrical profession may protest as much as it likes, the theologians may protest, and the majority of those who see our plays would probably be amazed to hear it, but the theatre is a religious institution devoted entirely to the exaltation of the spirit of man. It is an attempt to justify, not the ways of God to man, but the ways of man to himself. It is an attempt to prove that man has a dignity and a destiny, that his life is worth living, that he is not purely animal and without purpose. There is no doubt in my mind that our theatre, instead of being, as the evangelical ministers used to believe, the gateway to hell, is as much of a worship as the theatre of the Greeks, and has exactly the same meaning in our lives.

When I first wrote plays this statement would have seemed incredible to me. Broadway in the twenties, in the thirties, and now in 1941, has always worn an air of hard, garish, cheap professionalism. The lights, the glassy box-office men, the ornate and dirty buildings, the brokers, the groups of actors lingering in drugstores and along side streets, these all proclaim clearly a place of entertainment for sale. The priests and priestesses of these temples are certainly unaware of the nature of their profession. But consider what they sell, and you face a different prospect. The plays that please most and run longest in these sin-haunted alleys are representative of human loyalty, courage, love that purges the soul, grief that ennobles. Sometimes a simple tale like *Victoria Regina,* the story of a young girl faced suddenly with the responsibilities of an empire, unequal at first to the task, but developing and learning with the years, acquiring tolerance, wisdom and dignity, dying a great queen. Perhaps the story of Abraham Lincoln, a man with great endowments but afraid of life, forcing himself to face life, forcing himself to lead a nation in a war that sickened his soul, emerging at the end a great man. For those to whom this theory is novel it will seem easy to refute. The case of *Rain* will come up, where the uncritical tolerance and good will of a prostitute are held better moral guides than the fanatical zeal of the missionary. They are better moral guides, no doubt of it. But the play does not praise the woman for being a prostitute. It finds virtue in her despite her vocation. It does not condemn the man for his religion, but for the perversion of religion into an evil force. The case of *Tobacco Road* will come up, in which a poor white family struggles with a burden of poverty, ignorance and adverse social conditions. There is no doubt that the run of the play was stimulated by a morbid curiosity concerning the unashamed sexual customs of the inhabitants of that mythical road through the tobacco fields, but if there had been no moral values in the piece nobody would have cared to see it. The sexual customs or lack of them wouldn't have drawn a nickel. There were heroic qualities in Jeeter Lester and his strange brood. They lacked many virtues. They were shiftless, dishonest, financially hopeless. But they were not afraid. They faced existence as it was handed out to them in a way that made them both pathetic and tragic. Nothing better is expected of any hero on the stage than this—that he take up what arms he has against what enemies assail him and come out of the battle with his morale intact. Jeeter Lester kept very little except his self-respect, but he did keep that, and those who saw him had a respect both for him and for the human spirit that cannot be quenched by squalor. I have witnessed several plays on Broadway that attempted to imitate *Tobacco Road* by duplicating the adverse conditions and the resultant twisted lives and depressed morals. But they were failures because they assumed that the public wanted only dirt. It wasn't the dirt of *Tobacco Road* that gave it a long run, but the accompanying, and to many invisible, gallantry of its people.

Perhaps I have made my point nauseatingly clear, but I should like to present a little more evidence. As everybody knows, the great plays of the world—those accepted by civilization as part of a great heritage and played for centuries—these are almost all concerned with the conduct of exceptional men or women in positions of great responsibility, men with tragic faults and weaknesses but with mind and strength enough to overcome in the struggle with evil forces, both those within themselves and those without. This is *Hamlet, The Cid, Prometheus.* And it is also, please note, *Abe Lincoln in Illinois.* In such cases it is obvious that some kind of religious ritual is involved in reviving these symbols of national or cultural faith in a public performance. The *Oresteia* of Aeschylus is a ritual of crime and punishment, and ends by stating that Zeus himself must grow and learn and change if he is to avoid injustice. But here again we have a modern instance. *The Green Pastures* treats exactly the same theme, God's justice, and ends with exactly the same lesson, that God must learn and grow and change or his rigid justice will become an injustice in the end. I am fairly certain that Marc Connelly did not intentionally preach from the text of Aeschylus, but his play is no less a religious observance because it was presented in a plush-chaired theatre off our own gaudy Broadway. The worshippers pay a fairly high rent for their pews in the theatrical forties, and not many of them realize that they are assisting in a worship, but they sit in church nevertheless, and acquire virtue thereby according to their understanding and the wisdom and skill of the functioning playwright. *Oedipus Tyrannus* and *Macbeth* and *Little Eyolf* and *The Little Foxes* teach one and all that an evil action revenges itself upon the doer. *Antigone* and *Hamlet* and ten thousand modern plays argue that injustice is a corrosive, and will eat the heart out of him who practices it. Analyze any play you please which has survived the test of continued favor, and you will find a moral or a rule of social conduct or a rule of thumb which the race has considered valuable enough to learn and pass along. Take such seemingly meaningless escapades as *You Can't Take It with You* and *The Time of Your Life*. The first says simply that money isn't everything, and the second says, as plainly as the author can speak, that tolerance is the great virtue. These are platitudes, of course. A play is not required to make ethical discoveries. It is only required to have a meaning, and a sound one. One, that is, which is accepted as sound by its audience. Put on a play which sets out to prove that dishonesty is the best policy and vice is triumphant in human affairs, and the audience will refuse it coldly. They don't want to believe it and they won't.

They will believe and accept joyously a play that pokes

farcical fun at the virtues, so long as it's perfectly understood that both the playwright and the spectators are taking a brief vacation from the codes by which they live. In this we follow the Greeks, who seem to have anticipated us everywhere. For every heroic trilogy the playwrights of Athens wrote a satyric afterpiece—and so far as we can judge from the scanty remains this mocking fourth section held up to savage laughter the nobility and the high seriousness of all that had come before. The Greeks never fell into the error of the Puritans. They knew that man must remember from time to time that he is an animal, must sink to the flesh-pots, must subject the best that is in him to sardonic and impious inspection. They knew too that neither a religion nor a virtue is much good if such attacks can injure them, that it's healthy to subject our fundamental beliefs to the acid test of ribald laughter. It's just as healthy now as then to ventilate filthy rooms and comment pungently on pious attitudes. And so there is a place in the dramatic scheme for *The Playboy of the Western World,* in which murder is a fine thing, for *Arsenic and Old Lace,* in which murder is a minor foible, for *The Beggar's Opera,* in which the hero is a footpad, and for *Pal Joey* in which the hero is a rat. But there would be no place for them if there were any doubt what kind of plays they were. The audience must know—must be told by the author's attitude—that he is fooling—that this is the anti-mask, the corrective, the burlesque. If he tries to be serious in such matters no audience will follow him.

There have been critics who held that the theatre was central among the arts because it is a synthesis of all of them. Now I confess that the theatre appears to me to be the central art—but for a different reason. It does bring together all the arts, or a number of them. But its distinction is that it brings them together in a communal religious service. Any other art, practised separately, can be either moral or amoral, religious or pagan, affirmative or despairing. But when they come together in the theatre they must affirm, they cannot deny. It is as if poetry, music, narration, dancing and the mimetic arts were bits and pieces of theatrical art, stripped away to function alone, and rudderless without the moral compulsion of the theatre.

And now I must give a definition of what seems to me morally sound. If an artist believes that there is good and that there is evil, and in his work favors what seems to him good, and expects ultimate victory for it, then he is morally sound. If he does not believe in the existence of good and evil, or if, believing in them, he asks, or even anticipates, the triumph of evil, he is morally unsound. To some artists the present good may seem evil and the present evil good. That has happened often in the case of a poet or a prophet. A playwright cannot run so far ahead of his audience, for he must find a common denominator of his belief in his own generation, and even the greatest, the loftiest, must say something which his age can understand.

In brief, I have found my religion in the theatre, where I least expected to find it, and where few will credit that it exists. But it is there, and any man among you who tries to write plays will find himself serving it, if only because he can succeed in no other way. He will discover, if he works through his apprenticeship, that the theatre is the central artistic symbol of the struggle of good and evil within men. Its teaching is that the struggle is eternal and unremitting, that the forces which tend to drag men down are always present, always ready to attack, that the forces which make for good cannot sleep through a night without danger. It denies the doctrine of the nineteen-twenties emphatically. It denies that good and evil are obverse and reverse of the same coin, denies that good can win by waiting. It denies that wars are useless and that honor is without meaning. It denies that we can live by the laboratory and without virtue. It affirms that the good and evil in men are the good and evil of evolution, that men have within themselves the beasts from which they descend and the gōd toward which they climb. It affirms that evil is what takes man back toward the beast, that good is what urges him up toward the god. It affirms that these struggles of the spirit are enacted in the historic struggles of men—some representing evil, some good. It offers us criteria for deciding what is good and what is evil. Set a man on the stage and you know instantly where he stands morally with the race. Set Hitler on the stage and loathing will rise from every seat in the house. Even in Germany, if he were a character in a play, he would be hated and despised. Even in Germany, you cannot be pitiless, merciless, ruthless, arrogant and without God on the stage, and be considered a hero. Let the author of *The Wave of the Future* be warned, let Mr. Lindbergh and Senator Wheeler be warned; that which is considered despicable on the stage will be held despicable in real life—not only evil but those who will not fight evil are hated on the stage. A man who accepts the wave of the future and analyzes honor to a breath can be the comedian to be laughed at but he cannot be the protagonist. According to the worshippers of the good who sit in our theatres a hero may have his doubts and indecisions, for that's only human, but when it comes to the test he must be willing to take steel in his bosom or take lead through his intestines or he resigns his position as a man. The audience, sitting in our theatres, makes these rules and, in setting them, defines the purposes and beliefs of homo sapiens. There is no comparable test that I know of for what is good in the human soul, what is most likely to lead to that distant and secret destination which the race has chosen for itself and will somehow find.

M.A.

New City, Rockland County, N.Y.
October, 1941

CANDLE IN THE WIND had its first performance on any stage, in the Colonial Theatre, Boston, Mass., on Monday, September 15, 1941, when the drama was produced by The Theatre Guild, Inc., and The Playwrights' Company. The cast follows, in order of appearance.

FARGEAU	*Philip White*
HENRI	*Benedict MacQuarrie*
DESEZE	*Robert Harrison*
CHARLOTTE	*Leona Roberts*
MERCY	*Nell Harrison*
MADELINE GUEST	*Helen Hayes*
MAISIE TOMPKINS	*Evelyn Varden*
RAOUL ST. CLOUD	*Louis Borell*
GERMAN CAPTAIN	*Harro Meller*
GERMAN LIEUTENANT	*Knud Krueger*
COL. ERFURT	*John Wengraf*
LIEUT. SCHOEN	*Tonio Selwart*
CORPORAL BEHRENS	*Mario Gang*
MADAME FLEURY	*Michelette Burani*
M. FLEURY	*Stanley Jessup*
1ST GUARD	*Brian Connaught*
2ND GUARD	*Ferdi Hoffman*
CISSIE	*Lotte Lenya*
CORP. SHULZ	*Joseph Wiseman*
3RD GUARD	*George Andre*
4TH GUARD	*Guy Monypenny*
5TH GUARD	*William Malten*
CAPTAIN	*Bruce Fernald*

CANDLE IN THE WIND

ACT ONE

Act One

SCENE: A corner of the gardens behind the palace at Versailles. A number of high box hedges seclude the place. A flight of steps runs upstage. It is very early morning, sometime in September, 1940. FARGEAU, a workman, sits on the steps, reading a newspaper. HENRI, broom in hand, stands beside FARGEAU, looking over his shoulder.

Fargeau. Impossible! They are not Frenchmen! They are not men! They are—
[*Slaps the paper*]

Henri. They are politicians.

Fargeau. If the state could act—if it could carry through a policy—

Henri. It would not help much to act now.

Fargeau. Oh, God—let our memory perish—but let France be free!
[DESEZE, *a park attendant, enters.*]

Deseze. Henri! Move around! Circulate! Are you going to sweep all day in one spot?

Henri. He reads the decrees to me, the decrees of Paris.

Deseze. You sweep in one spot because you wait for a pourboire, I know that well enough.

Henri. And why do you carry chairs so early in the morning? For the same lady and her pourboire!

Fargeau.

[*Throwing down paper*]

Traitors!

Deseze. There is too much said of traitors. Who are the traitors now?

Fargeau. Whoever writes these things! The reporters, the journalists, the editors! The dirty liars and traitors!

Deseze. Do you have a test for truth and falsehood, little Fargeau?

Fargeau. I say every fool knows the Germans sit in the offices with guns and say what must be written!

Deseze. There's no law that a man must read it. What do they say this morning?

Fargeau. Look at it! Take it in! Mix it with your breakfast if you can! "German Forces Occupy All France. Little Resistance Offered."

Deseze. Yes, God help us; it's true.

Fargeau. I tell you they should be shot down, the traitors who write such things, and those who print them!

Deseze. The journalists are merely the historians of the present, my dear Fargeau. They write what exists. They can hardly choose.

Fargeau. Why, you fool, do you believe these lies? This is all the doing of the secret agents! This is how they win! Up in Belgium their secret agents ran through the villages crying, "All is lost! Fly! The Germans have broken through! They are butchering the peasants!" And the peasants believed them, and clogged the roads—and the nation was destroyed! And now you believe them!

Deseze. We saw them take Paris and march on south. It's not difficult to believe the rest.

Fargeau. I know they took Paris. They can take a city! They have done that before. But France is not taken in a day nor a week! Nor in a hundred years!

Henri. My son came home from the south last night.

Deseze. He was discharged?

Henri. He was lost from his company. He says there is now no army of France, even in the south. No army, no command, no line of battle. The men are going home.

Fargeau. Do you know what I would do if I believed that? I would kill a few of these Germans.

Henri. It's true.

Deseze. Yes, it's true, and you will kill nobody.
[*A German* CAPTAIN *is heard speaking off stage.*]

Captain. Schoener Morgen heute!
[CAPTAIN *and* LIEUTENANT *enter and start to pass through.*]

Lieutenant. Ja! Wenn wir uns beeilen, können wir das Trianon bis mittag besichtigt haben.

Captain. Ich muss sagen Potsdam interessiert mich mehr.

Lieutenant. Dem Baedecker nach müssten wir auf dem

rechten Wege sein! I beg your pardon, this is the way to the Trianon?

[DESEZE *does not answer.*]

Is this the way to the Trianon?

Deseze. Yes.

Lieutenant. Danke.
Finden Sie es denn nicht huebsch hier?

Captain. Ja, nur die Zustaende gefallen mir garnicht.

Lieutenant.
[*As they go toward the exit*]
Ich verstehe nicht was sie daran auszusetzen haben.

Captain. Rennen Sie doch nicht so. Wir haben doch Zeit.
[*They go out.*]

Lieutenant.
[*Off stage*]
Beeilen Sie sich schon, wir wollen doch bis zwei Uhr zurueck sein.

Fargeau. Yes, I would kill one or two of them. I'm too old for many things, but not too old to die. Better to die, if thereby France is free.

Deseze. The gates are open, go find your mop and bucket.
[FARGEAU *goes out.*]
[CHARLOTTE *and* MERCY *enter.*]

Charlotte. Sister!

Mercy. Yes, Charlotte.

Charlotte. I have found a park attendant—one who looks intelligent.

Mercy. Oh, yes! Oh, if you please—
  [DESEZE *turns, looking up to them.*]

Deseze. Yes, madame?

Mercy. Perhaps you would be willing to help us. We are attempting to reconstruct the past, with the most inadequate evidence.

Deseze. To reconstruct the past?

Mercy. Yes.

Deseze. Madame, I wish you all success.

Charlotte. But we need assistance desperately!

Deseze. For that project you do indeed!

Charlotte. It's only—there was once a lake here at Versailles. Lilies grew at the margin, mingled with sedge, and large swans floated about on its surface. Can you tell us where it was?

Deseze. When was that lake here, madame?

Charlotte. In the time of Louis XVI.

Deseze. I fear I cannot help you. Ancient as I appear, and old as is my uniform, my recollection stops this side of Louis XVI.

Charlotte. Oh, and so does ours, so does ours.

Deseze. I have not yet finished the morning routine, so if you will excuse me—

Mercy. Please listen. We are school teachers from New Hampshire, and for many years we have made a study of the life of Marie Antoinette. We have read and re-

read the memoirs of her life, and we have pored over all the available maps and pictures of the period. Now at last we have saved enough to visit the shrines of our interest. But here at Versailles, we are utterly disappointed.

Deseze. Will you tell me why, madame?

Charlotte. Because it's been changed! It's not as it was in the days of Louis XVI.

Deseze. Naturally!

Mercy. But if we could place the lake, we could use it as a key, and then we could locate accurately all the missing features of that old landscape.—

Charlotte. And then we thought perhaps the government would help to reconstruct it as it was—so that travellers from far away could enter here and look back into that beautiful old world.

Mercy. So that modern men and women could see these gardens as they appeared to Marie Antoinette, when she walked among the orange trees long ago!

Deseze. The whole earth is at war, mesdames. All nations are in danger, and mine is already over-run. The Germans take Paris and pour down to the Pyrenees, and you hunt for the ghost of Marie Antoinette, in the gardens of Versailles!

Mercy. He doesn't understand.

Charlotte. But how could he?

Mercy. No, it couldn't be expected.

Charlotte. No. Have you the map, my dear?

Mercy. Yes, here it is.

Charlotte. We will have to proceed with our search alone.
   [*They go out.*]

Maisie.
   [*Off stage*]
   Madeline—Madeline—
   [MADELINE *runs on from the right, and down the steps.*]

Deseze. Good morning, mademoiselle.

Madeline. Good morning, Deseze.—Will you do something for me?

Deseze. Yes, mademoiselle.

Madeline. There is a tall and broad American woman entering by the gate just above, wearing a green cape. If she asks for me, will you say that I have gone toward the palace?

Deseze. Yes, of course, mademoiselle.

Madeline. Thank you!
   [*She gives him a coin.*]

Deseze.
   [*Going up the steps*]
   Merci. You are early this morning.

Madeline. Yes.
   [*She sits, concealing her face.*]

Deseze. It's a beautiful morning, that's one thing the Germans haven't taken from us.
   [*He meets* MAISIE.]
   If you will forgive me, madame.

Maisie. Excusez-moi—mais avez vous voyez une dame passez par ici—Oh! C'est la. Il n'ya pas de quoi. Depechez vous, vite!

[*She avoids* Deseze *and goes toward the stairs.*]

Three years in Paris, and that's the best I can do!

[*She sits on the bench beside* Madeline.]

Madeline! It is Madeline!

Madeline. Maisie! Oh, Maisie, my dear! I thought I heard someone calling—

Maisie. Don't apologize, and I won't.

Madeline. For what?

Maisie. You ran like hell when you saw me.

Madeline. I ran from you?

Maisie. Yes, ma cherie, but I ran like hell after you, so we're even. Darling, I sold you that dress, and as for your figure, I know it as well going away as coming toward. It hasn't changed since high school!

Madeline. I could say I didn't recognize you.

Maisie. I'm also unmistakable. Look at my proportions. You knew me, lady. You had a reason?

Madeline. I thought I had.

Maisie. Shall I go?

Madeline. But now that you're here, please stay if you can. I haven't seen a familiar face in months.

Maisie. I do apologize, darling. You should be allowed to live your own life. But you left Paris four months ago, you know.

Madeline. Yes, I remember.

Maisie. Left for New York in a shower of headlines. I saw you off on the boat-train myself.

Madeline. Yes I remember that, too.

Maisie. Now I catch a glimpse of you, calmly strolling down an avenue in Versailles. Do you wonder I gave chase?

Madeline. I must be fascinating.

Maisie. You are. You meant to disappear?

Madeline. In a way.

Maisie. Did you do something unprintable?

Madeline. I'd rather it wasn't printed.

Maisie. Oh well, I won't repeat it.

Madeline. No. I'm sure you won't.

Maisie. You're not saying?

Madeline. No.

Maisie.
    [*Starts to rise*]
    Now I really should go.

Madeline. No, Maisie! Stay if you can! It's such a relief to talk to someone I know. Oh, this horrible, horrible news, Maisie! And these sickening Germans! They're everywhere! They're even here!

Maisie. Yes, I got up early this morning to say good-bye.

Madeline. Good-bye?

Maisie. To Paris and the things I've loved here. We may never see them again.

Madeline. Can they make France a province?

Maisie. I only know what the correspondents say in the Ritz Bar. Some maintain that conquest can't be permanent—that it's only skin deep. Others say that this is the beginning of the new ice age, and the Nazis are coming down like a snow cap over civilization. As for Americans, they were given their last warning months ago.

Madeline. And you're going tomorrow?

Maisie. Going tomorrow. I've been saying that for two weeks now, but this time I really mean it. Business loyalty is all very well, but I simply can't face the prospect of fitting a Berlin hausfrau into a Paris model! There's something fundamentally wrong with the combination. And I mean fundamentally. So—tomorrow I sever my very profitable connection with Nicolet et Cie. If I can get a seat on a plane. If I can get two, will you come with me?

Madeline. I can't.

Maisie. Obligations?

Madeline. I just can't.

Maisie. Well, I'm not exactly a psychologist, my dear—but I should say there was only one answer. You're suffering from a madness peculiar to women—you've fallen in love.

Madeline. Peculiar to women?

Maisie. I see. You believe he loves you in return. Well,

that may be true in rare instances. I've never known a case.

Madeline. You're probing.
[*She rises, and goes up the steps, looking about.*]

Maisie. I guess I'm clumsy with a probe, but I've been worried about you a little—

Madeline. Oh?

Maisie. Well, we ran through our fifteens and twenties together, Madeline.—The reason I'm so familiar with your back is that I've watched you so often walking away with the young man I wanted. Then we went on the stage together, and you walked away with the parts I wanted. Now I'm selling frocks and you're a star, and I still see you through a rosy mist of adoration.

Madeline. Maisie, Maisie—you were always an angel.

Maisie. By Rubens, I know. So, if you're in love, out with it, and if he's a no-good like the first one I'll tell you.

Madeline. You guessed this much—that I fell in love.

Maisie. You can tell me how, even if you can't tell me who.

Madeline. How?

Maisie. I saw you start off on that boat-train, darling, and your destination was in all the papers. How did you get here?

Madeline. I got off the ship.

Maisie. They won't let you.

Madeline. Well, they did, I paid them.

Maisie. Impulse, or malice aforethought?

Madeline. I may as well tell you the whole story.

Maisie. That's right, darling.

Madeline.

[*Sitting on the balustrade*]

Well, it started with that radio Midas in New York—who wanted to marry me. Rich as the Mint, very smooth.

Maisie. Like a soap commercial on the air.

Madeline. Yes. Well, the theory is that an actress ought to marry money while she can, and I was tempted.

Maisie. Tired of trooping?

Madeline. No, it wasn't that I wanted to quit the theatre. It was just that—when once you've been poor a multi-millionaire has a special glamor for you. We scrimped so hard in that 47th Street room that I used to dream of finding money. In great piles and fortunes. Security forever, even when you're old. And the radio man was very nice, and everything he touched turned to gold, so I was tempted. But something warned me to think it over, so I came to Paris to think.

Maisie. Some other city might have been better. So, while you were thinking?

Madeline. Yes.

Maisie. Perhaps I saw you about with him once or twice. He wore an officer's uniform, and once you rode in the Bois?

Madeline. Possibly.

Maisie. Very sudden, no doubt?

Madeline. I don't know. I went to the Comédie Française one night and an officer sat beside me. He lent me his opera glasses, and walked to my hotel with me afterward. That was all—nothing romantic, nothing said. Only I went to Molière again the next night, and so did he.

Maisie. Is he handsome?

Madeline. I don't know.—I don't know.

Maisie. O, dear—this is serious.

Madeline. We saw more and more of each other. Then, before long, we were seeing nobody else. I told myself that this would never do, so I took passage away on the *Saturnia.* I stood on the boat deck, and watched the Mediterranean waters open between me and the pier. Then I knew I couldn't leave France, so I opened negotiations with the pilot. Next morning I was back in Paris. I came here—and Raoul was here. Did you know that this was an enchanted place for lovers, this corner of the gardens? Raoul told me the legend. Lost things are found here. And if a woman waits here, and wishes hard enough, her lover will turn, wherever he is, and come this way.

Maisie. I'm not superstitious. Well, it's made one alteration in you. In New York I never knew you to rise before noon.
[*She looks at her watch.*]
Exactly 6:30 A.M.

Madeline. I know. I can't sleep.
  [*She rises, looking about.*]
  So I get up and come here, hoping.

Maisie. There came an end to this idyll?

Madeline. Yes, he was on leave.

Maisie. This is a hell of a time to fall in love with a French officer.

Madeline. He's a journalist really. He was in the naval reserve.

Maisie. Raoul?

Madeline. Yes.

Maisie. Nice name. But it must be Raoul St. Cloud.

Madeline. Yes, it is.

Maisie. I didn't know you went in for politics.

Madeline. I don't.

Maisie. But St. Cloud writes political comment for *L'Evangile.* The best written in Paris. Don't you read it?

Madeline. I do now.

Maisie. He certainly told the Germans what an honest man thinks about them. I hope he's not among the absent or missing.

Madeline. He is, though.

Maisie. Darling, you'd better let go and come back to America with me.

Madeline. Why?

Maisie. They say very few will come out of those prison camps, and those few won't be all in one piece.

Madeline. I think he'll come back.

Maisie. Have you heard from him since he left?

Madeline. Yes. His destroyer was used as a transport to take men out of Dunkirk. Since then I haven't heard. [*She sits.*]

Maisie. You haven't? Well he may have come through Dunkirk, some did.

Madeline. For God's sake, Maisie, I hate staying here! I've thought of all this! What do you suppose I think about sitting alone in an empty park? I don't want to be caught and trapped and helpless. But there's nothing I can do. I can't go—I have to stay.

Maisie. My sweet, I'd better leave you. I've run into something holy here. I'm treading on sacred ground, and I'll get out.

Madeline. Don't be silly.

Maisie. Maybe you don't know what's happened to you. Maybe you've never been in love before.

Madeline. Maybe not. It feels as if maybe not. Oh, Maisie —you know how it is. You can be a little in love, and that's fun—and you can be deep in love, so that you think of him first in the morning and last at night, and that's wonderful. But this time—it isn't fun, and it isn't wonderful—it's—oh, darling, when he's gone life's one endless misery—and he's been gone so long!

Maisie. My sweet, if I leave you here, it's like leaving a drunk on a railroad track.

Madeline. I know I should go. I've known it all the time. There's no hope—and yet beyond reason I keep on hoping. My mind tells me right now, if you love your life go with Maisie.

Maisie. Then you have some sense left, and in the end you'll come.

[RAOUL *appears above in the distance.*]

Madeline. Maisie—

Maisie. Yes?

Madeline. There.

Maisie. It's—

Madeline. Yes.

Maisie. The Gods are with you. Where are you stopping?

Madeline. Plaza Athene—

Maisie. If I had a tail, it would hang in the traditional position—and if an elephant can slink, I'm slinking.

[*She goes out.* RAOUL *enters and stands for a moment motionless.*]

Madeline. I'd come toward you, but I can't move. Did you go to the hotel?

Raoul. I didn't dare venture there. I hoped you'd be here.

Madeline. You're not wounded?

Raoul. No. Did you pray for me?

Madeline. Yes.

Raoul. I knew you must have. I've been through miracles. I've prayed to you so long, from so many unimaginable places, I must worship you a moment before I touch you. I think there must be a God.

Madeline. There must be: I was afraid your ship was lost.

Raoul. It was.

Madeline. They said it would be impossible for a man to come through free and alive.

Raoul. Yes, it was impossible, that's how I knew you prayed.

Madeline. Let me look at you.—
　　[*She goes near him, then into his arms.*]

Raoul. How I have wanted you!

Madeline. How I have wanted you!

Raoul. I'd have died in the sea if it hadn't been for you. How did you do it, darling?

Madeline. You had time to think of me?

Raoul. Every time it got desperate, I found I was thinking of you—and that saved me. You were a goddess, with your hand stretched over me.—I could feel you there, saving my life.—But I can't stay here. There may be mopping up operations.

Madeline. I didn't know there was fighting still!

Raoul. Here and there, where men are stubborn.
　　[HENRI *enters.* RAOUL *wheels around, about to draw his automatic.* MADELINE *puts her hand on his arm to restrain him.*]

Madeline. It's all right, Raoul. Oh, Henri—

Henri. Yes, mademoiselle?

Madeline. Are there German soldiers about?

Henri. Only the two in the Trianon.

Madeline. If they come near will you let us know?

Henri. Yes, mademoiselle.

Raoul. You know him?

Madeline. Henri? He's an old friend. He'll keep good watch.
[HENRI *goes out.* RAOUL *puts a hand over his eyes.*]
Darling, what is it?

Raoul. Don't laugh. But I'm probably still a little drunk.

Madeline. Drunk?

Raoul. You see, when I came out of the ocean I was as blue as a mackerel. And they poured me full of hot rum, and thawed me out in the engine room—so if I sound a little maudlin—or stumble a little—

Madeline. I'm a little drunk myself just with seeing you, so I wouldn't notice. But maybe you'd better sit down, darling.
[*They sit.*]
How did you get here?

Raoul. By plane. We happened to steal a plane, another man and I. It was a German plane.

Madeline. But how could you?

Raoul. It was quite illogical, like everything else these days. And we were all pretty desperate, too.

Madeline. But these are not your clothes.

Raoul. No, I came naked out of the sea this morning. An officer lent me these things. You see, our captain refused to surrender when the Germans took over the port, and the destroyer fought a lonely battle against four submarines. I don't know quite what we did to them, but in the end they sank us. Somewhere around the middle of the Channel. That was—why that was yesterday!

Madeline. You say these things so calmly!

Raoul. I was a little nervous at the time. After they sank us, well it was dark, nothing to be seen but black sky and black ocean—and I was alone in it. Don't tell me you didn't pull me through that, because I know. A man can swim just so long in a frigid sea with water chopping over him and no notion of east or west. I got rid of my clothes, and my coat, with the one letter I ever had from you—then I lost my precious piece of plank and had nothing to cling to—so I clung to you, darling, just to you, and without you I'd be frozen and drowned and dead!

Madeline. It's unfair that men go through such things, and women can't help them.

Raoul. But you haven't listened! You couldn't have helped more with a lifeline! And it wasn't only that once! It was many times I'd have gone down into some blackness, but then the thought of you would nerve me up, and I'd make a decision, and take courage, and stumble on. It was always the right way—always the one thing that would have saved me, always that miracle. You know I'm sane enough; I like to see things as they are. But coming straight out of it this way, with no sleep and no breakfast, it seems like more than mortal.

Madeline. No breakfast—come.

[*She rises.*]

Raoul.

[*Taking her in his arms*]

No, not yet—don't go yet—it won't matter—I'm a bit irregular in my habits, anyway—lately. One meal a week like an anaconda.

Madeline. But there's a restaurant nearby, where I can get coffee and croissants. So, please—

Raoul. What I need most of all is a change of clothes. You see, in these I can't go anywhere—

Madeline. I'll try.

Raoul. Just anything—any workman's clothes.

Madeline.

[*Going toward the steps*]

Can you wait here in the park?

Raoul. I'll have to chance it.

[*She turns.*]

Are the wires still working, darling?

Madeline. I think so. Do you want me to send a message?

Raoul. I have it written out here. It's a private code. But what it says is that I'll be in Dijon tomorrow.

Madeline. In Dijon?

Raoul. A few of us are starting south tomorrow to try to find the French fleet. We still have a fleet, you know, though we have no country.

Madeline. But the war's ended!

Raoul. Not for me, dear, not for any of us who isn't helpless.

Madeline. No—no.—What do you mean?

Raoul. Madeline darling, I must go back.

Madeline. Go back?

Raoul. Yes, dear—

Madeline. Into the war?

Raoul. Yes, somehow—with what weight I have—with whatever I can do—

Madeline. When?

Raoul. I've promised to leave tomorrow.

Madeline. Then you haven't come back at all!

Raoul. Oh, darling, you just don't know the difference between today and nothing. Between one night more and death in the sea.

Madeline.
   [*Sitting*]
   Raoul?

Raoul. Yes?

Madeline. Sitting here waiting, it seemed mad to hope that you would come at all. But not once did I ever imagine anything so mad as that you would come—and then go back into it. What good will more dying do?

Raoul. I count on you—to keep me from dying.

Madeline. Then I have no part in the decision—and nothing to say?

Raoul. If you were to choose my course, dear, and your one voice decided, what would you say then?

Madeline. I'd say come with me.

Raoul. Where, dear?

Madeline. Anywhere, away from here.

Raoul. To your country?

Madeline. Yes, if you wouldn't mind.

Raoul. I think I'd love your country, because it's yours. But it's not mine. What if America were sometime in desperate straits, and the men of America ran away? What would you think of them?

Madeline. I don't know.

Raoul. Yes, you do know. Every woman knows the answer to that.

Madeline. Yes, I suppose so.

Raoul.

[*His hands on her shoulders*]

We fell in love so quickly—we were so sure of each other—that I hardly paused to think of what world you came out of—or you to question mine. Now we face these things sharply, in an hour of battle. I am a Frenchman—and fight for France. For many years I

· 24 ·

fought with my pen against them, but not well enough. Not well enough, darling, and so now we must all fight as we can—desperately—with whatever arms there are.

Madeline. Oh, I wonder—I wonder—how many chances we're given! Have you ever dreamed that the face of the earth had changed—and you were lost in a world you didn't know?

Raoul. Not quite that.

Madeline. It's been a nightmare with me lately. Sometimes it came to me as I sat there in the park to wait for you—the streets all different, nothing familiar—rivers and roads change places—the maps are all wrong, and I'm alone in the world—searching over this unknown landscape for you. We're to meet at Versailles—but there's no way to find it.

Raoul. Yes, last night was like that.

Madeline. And then what if it's so long and so cruel, and the iron cuts so deep, that we change too? It's such a fragile thing, the meeting of lovers. There must be a place and a time for them to meet—and they must somehow stay alive and somehow reach that tiny focus in eternity which is all they have. And they must want to find each other—the flame must survive the wind. How do we dare part, Raoul, knowing how all the chances are against us?

Raoul. Most of the lovers of the world are parting just that way these days.

Madeline. But those lovers have no gulf between them! Oh, Raoul, Raoul, you're willing to die for something

I don't understand! And that comes between us!

Raoul. You'd die for it too, if it came to a choice.

Madeline. I, Raoul? What would I die for?

Raoul. Rather than live ignobly.

Madeline. I don't know.

Raoul. But I know. I saw you from a long way off—when I was there in the sea. And I know.

Madeline. You always do this to me. Make me believe in miracles.
[*They kiss.*]
I'll bring the breakfast, and what clothes I can find.
[*She goes up the steps.* Henri *enters.*]

Henri. Mademoiselle, monsieur—

Raoul. What is it?

Henri. You must hurry, sir, they're coming back—

Madeline. What have you seen?

Henri. They came so quickly, mademoiselle! They were not here, and then they were here. They have set guards at this exit. Forgive me, there is still time.
[*He goes out.*]

Raoul. Is there a guard at that gate?

Madeline. Yes.

Raoul. Perhaps this way—
[*He goes out to look and returns after a pause.*]
No—

Madeline. What can I do?

Raoul. You must walk rapidly to that exit—and turn right from it along the avenue—

Madeline. You'll fight with them?

Raoul. I don't know.

Madeline. But it's senseless to die this way!

Raoul. They may not find me—but if they do, it's this way or a labor camp, Madeline.

Madeline. But if you die! No, no, dear—if you're alive there's at least a chance! A chance to get free! A chance to live!

    [*She runs to him.*]

Even for France it's wrong to die! It's giving up, saying it's no use any more!

Lieutenant.

    [*Outside*]

Wissen Sie gestern abend war ich im Ball Tabarin, diese Maedchen dort das ist ja toll.

Captain.

    [*As he enters with the* LIEUTENANT]

Das Leben hier gefaellt mir so gut, dass ich nie mehr fort moechte.

    [CHARLOTTE *and* MERCY *appear.*]

Raoul. Sit a moment.

    [*He sits on the bench,* MADELINE *between him and the soldiers.*]

Captain. Na, das wird sich schön einrichten lassen, warum denn nicht?

Mercy. I grow more certain the lake lay here to the left.

Charlotte. I should have thought a little further on.

Lieutenant. Schauen Sie, sind das nicht Amerikaner?

Captain. Scheint so! Sonderbar, treiben die sich noch immer hier herum?

Lieutenant. Und dieser Mann da, in der Uniform, wollen wir doch mal sehen was der hier macht.

Captain. Das werden wir gleich haben.
> [*He goes down the steps.* MADELINE *rises.*]

Your pardon, sir; you wear the uniform of the French aviation forces?

Raoul. Yes, I do. It's not mine, however. I am a lieutenant in the navy.

Captain. May I see your papers?

Raoul. Unfortunately, I have not my papers with me.

Captain. Where are they?

Raoul. Somewhere in the shallow sea between France and England. I was forced to leave them there last night.

Captain. You will stand up, please.
> [RAOUL *rises.*]

This is very unfortunate. We are obliged to arrest all stragglers. We had hoped to find none, but unfortunately for both of us, you are here. Also, we have placed a patrol at each exit, and you will therefore not attempt to use your arms, for you are a sensible person. Your automatic, please.

Raoul.
> [*To* MADELINE]

This is a tame end for a soldier.
> [*Takes out his gun*]

Madeline. No, no, Raoul, you must listen to me. Please!
> [RAOUL *sees that he is covered by the* LIEUTENANT *and gives his gun to the* CAPTAIN.]

Raoul. For the moment.

Captain. You see, every man's luck runs out sometime.

Raoul. Even Hitler's?

Captain. We shall see.

Lieutenant. Das wird uns aufhalten.

Captain. Das macht ja nichts. Come on, this way.

Madeline. He's not serving against you! His ship was sunk; he's here only to see me!

Captain. I can well believe you, my dear.

Madeline. But you can't take him now! There's to be an armistice now. The war's ended! He's no danger to you, one in so many millions!

Captain. I'm sorry; we have our orders.

Madeline. Then we must have a few minutes—to say what must be said.

Captain. If there's nothing against him, he will be released tomorrow, my dear.

Madeline. You say that, but it's not true!

Captain. Will you show me your passport?
[*She takes the passport out of her bag, hands it to him.
He glances at it, and returns it to her.*]
An American?

Madeline. Yes.

Captain. This gentleman is in my custody, mademoiselle.
I prefer that there is no interference, no argument, no
outcry in the streets. Will you go quietly to your hotel,
or shall I detail a soldier to escort you?

Madeline. I will go quietly.

Captain. Good. Vorwaerts!

Madeline.
[*Taking* RAOUL's *arm*]
Darling, till I see you—

Raoul. Yes, Madeline—
[*He goes out with the soldiers.* MERCY *and* CHARLOTTE
enter above.]

Mercy. Charlotte! The soldiers—ask her if we can help
her—

Charlotte. Can we help you in any way, mademoiselle?

Mercy. If there's anything we can do—

Madeline. Thank you, no—there's nothing.
[*She goes out.*]

CURTAIN

· 30 ·

Act One

SCENE: A disused pumping station on the outskirts of Paris, now the office of a concentration camp. Within the concrete walls the Nazis have set up gates, barriers and run-ways built of new wood and heavy wire fencing. In the midst of this inferno a delicate chair and table have been set for the commandant, COLONEL ERFURT. ERFURT *is ensconced in the chair as the curtain rises, and* LIEUTENANT SCHOEN *sits at a plain table to the left.*

Erfurt. Are there others waiting who should be taken care of today?

Schoen. This list, sir, and a new guard sent from headquarters.

Erfurt. I will see the guard first and then the others.
[SCHOEN *rises, pushes a button on his desk, and crosses to* ERFURT *as a* GUARD *enters through the wire cage from the left.*]

Schoen.
[*To the* GUARD]
Corporal Behrens.
[*The* GUARD *goes out.*]

Guard.
[*Outside*]
Corporal Behrens!
[*The* GUARD *reenters, followed by* BEHRENS. SCHOEN *unlocks the gate, admitting* BEHRENS *into the room.*]

Schoen. This is Corporal Behrens, Colonel Erfurt, reporting for duty under orders. You have his commission.

Erfurt. Yes. In what specialty have you been trained, Corporal?

Behrens. In punishments, sir.

Erfurt. What punishments?

Behrens. In all degrees, sir.

Erfurt. You have had experience?

Behrens. Two years, sir.

Erfurt. You will take over the examination, Lieutenant.
[BEHRENS *turns to* SCHOEN.]

Schoen. Yes, sir. Why are men punished in the Third Reich?

Behrens. Because they are guilty.

Schoen. And how do you know they are guilty?

Behrens. Because they are condemned by the state, and the state makes no errors.

Schoen. If you discovered that the state had made an error, would you report it to the proper authorities?

Behrens. It is impossible, sir, that the state has made an error. In any conflict between the state and the individual, the state is right, and the individual is wrong.

Schoen. But suppose God whispers in a man's heart, and tells him truth, so that he is right, and the state is mistaken?

Behrens. It is impossible, sir. There is no God except the state, and the state carries out our Fuehrer's will.

Schoen. But suppose, for example, that you are right, and I am wrong?

Behrens. It is impossible, sir, because the state has set you above me in authority.

Erfurt. Good. Very good. You will assist with punishments in the third tier. Give this to the guard; he will conduct you.
> [BEHRENS *salutes. The* GUARD *opens the door and he goes out right.*]

Erfurt. We must make a census of the vacant cells in the reception tier. A consignment of prisoners arrives to-day. Transferred from unoccupied France.

Schoen. I took such a census yesterday, Colonel Erfurt. This report shows the cells vacant, and also those not used to capacity.

Erfurt. They appear to train you fellows well in Moabite. You anticipate me.

Schoen. I believe the system to be excellent in Berlin, sir.

Erfurt. Yes. However in the future you will kindly inform me before you proceed with such a matter.

Schoen. Yes, sir.

Erfurt. Besucher siebenundzwanzig und achtundzwanzig.
> [SCHOEN *pushes buzzer,* GUARD *appears in cage.*]

Schoen. Besucher siebenundzwanzig und achtundzwanzig.
> [*He unlocks the gate.*]

A Guard.
> [*Outside*]

Ausweiskarte vorzeigen—passiert!

[*A* GUARD *enters, followed by* MME. FLEURY *and* M. FLEURY.]

Guard. Folgen sie mir. Besucher siebenundzwanzig und achtundzwanzig.

Schoen. Your card.

[MME. FLEURY *hands him her card through the wire door.*]

M. and Mme. Fleury?

[*They nod.*]

Heil Hitler!

[*They lift their hands but do not speak.* SCHOEN *opens the gate.*]

Guard. Schnell! Schnell!

[*He pushes the* FLEURYS *into the room, and follows them.* SCHOEN *closes and relocks the gate.*]

Erfurt. Stuhl für die Frau.

[*The* GUARD *brings a stool, places* MME. FLEURY *on it.*]

Sit down.

Sachen abnehmen.

[*The* GUARD *takes her pocketbook.*]

Handschuhe.

[*The* GUARD *takes her gloves.*]

You have a son?

Mme. Fleury. Yes, sir.

Erfurt. How old is your son, Mme. Fleury.

Mme. Fleury. He is twenty-seven.

Erfurt. We had thought him older.

Mme. Fleury. Then I may see him?

Erfurt. You live at Tours?

Mme. Fleury. Yes, sir.

Erfurt. What is your position in the city of Tours?

Mme. Fleury. We are poor people, sir. My husband has a little farm.

Erfurt. Listen to me carefully. It is my custom to use kindness, but it is not my custom to repeat my words. This camp is here for a special purpose. It does not contain all grades and varieties of prisoners. We have here only political or philosophical offenders who have given us reason to believe them dangerous. It will not be possible for you to see your son.

Mme. Fleury. But he is the gentlest of men.

Erfurt. Of course. I know.

Mme. Fleury. M. Director, we have walked here this hundred miles, for there was no transport, even if we could pay, and we could not.

Erfurt. I'm sorry.

Mme. Fleury. We must go?

Erfurt. Yes. Unless there were some excuse for the interview.

Mme. Fleury. Excuse?

Erfurt. These are not my rules alone. Interviews are permitted only in the public interest. Would you be willing to ask your son a question?

Mme. Fleury. What question?

· 35 ·

Erfurt. Unfortunately, there is nothing your son can tell me which I do not know—but for form's sake ask him how you can communicate with him without the knowledge of the authorities.

Mme. Fleury. My son told us, never—even to save his life—we must never assist you.

Erfurt. Your son is ill—he is confined to his cot. He will be up and about in a few days, but he is ill. If you wish to see him—

Mme. Fleury. Yes, yes—we will ask the one question.

Erfurt. Good. Follow the guard, you will have fifteen minutes.

Mme. Fleury. Maybe—if he is ill—perhaps I could care for him a little, perhaps I could bring him food—

Erfurt. Maybe.

> [A Guard *ushers the* Fleurys *through the inner door.*]

Besucher neunundzwanzig.

Schoen.

> [*To a* Guard]

Besucher neunundzwanzig.

Guard.

> [*Off stage*]

Besucher neunundzwanzig.

Erfurt. Who is Madeline Guest?

Schoen. An American, sir.

> [*He lays a folder on* Erfurt's *desk.*]

I have made a digest of the available information concerning her, if you wish to see it.

Erfurt.
[*Examining the dossier*]
Oh yes, the American actress. I know the name. It is the American actress? You have made sure?

Schoen. Quite positive, sir. She has been here several times, and we have looked into her background.
[A GUARD *appears with* MADELINE *behind the wire barrier.*]

Guard. Besucher neunundzwanzig.
[*He goes out.*]

Schoen. May I see your card, please?
[MADELINE *hands him her card through wire door.*]
Your name is Madeline Guest?

Madeline. Yes.

Schoen. Heil Hitler!

Madeline. I have an appointment with Colonel Erfurt.

Schoen. The greeting is essential.

Madeline. I am an American citizen.

Schoen. It is still essential.

Madeline. I can't—no—

Erfurt. Don't be an ass, Lieutenant. Lassen Sie sie doch herein.
[SCHOEN *unlocks the gate.* MADELINE *enters.*]
You are really Madeline Guest?

Madeline. Yes.

Erfurt. The American actress?

Madeline. Yes.

Erfurt. It's incredible. Now how in the world would you happen to be here?

Madeline. You've heard of me?

Erfurt. I have indeed. That's why it's incredible. There is a certain incongruity of associations. Please—
   [*He offers her the stool.* Schoen *shuts the gate.*]
You have come to examine us?

Madeline. No.

Erfurt. There is someone here—in whom you take an interest?

Madeline. Yes.

Erfurt. What evil fortune. Good for us, for it brings you here, but bad for those who have friends within.

Madeline. Always?

Erfurt. No, forgive me, not always. No, sometimes wisdom penetrates the walls and the bird is free.

Madeline. You make it sound easy.

Erfurt. It is easy. And I assure you, Miss Guest, I shall be as helpful as I can. Come, sit down.—
   [Madeline *sits.*]
What mortal man has so mingled good luck and bad as to be here and bring you here to seek him?

Madeline. I have come to ask permission to visit a prisoner who is held here.

Erfurt. Yes?

Madeline. Raoul St. Cloud. I think I have filled out all the necessary forms.

Erfurt. Yes, indeed you have. You are not related to this gentleman?

Madeline. You will find that answered in the questionnaire, I think. No, I'm not.

Erfurt. You wish to see him for sentimental reasons?

Madeline. I wish to see him.

Erfurt. Are you married, Miss Guest?

Madeline. No, I am not.

Erfurt. You have a romantic interest in the gentleman in question?

Madeline. I would rather not answer you.

Erfurt. Why? Do tell me why.

Madeline. It seems to me that any answer I might make in this place, and to you, would lessen both him and me.

Erfurt. Yes, perhaps. Yes—I see. I will put the question another way. You would make sacrifices to see M. St. Cloud? Important sacrifices?

Madeline. Yes.

Erfurt. I think this answer may be regarded as satisfactory.

Madeline. He is here?

Erfurt. St. Cloud?

Madeline. Yes.

Erfurt. Yes, Raoul St. Cloud is here.

Madeline. May I see him?

Erfurt. I am not entirely a free agent, Miss Guest. There are rules. I must look into the case a little further before I can answer that question. And a little earlier or later in the day doesn't matter. Or does it?

Madeline. Yes, it does matter.

Erfurt. I should have thought the lover would reflect: The sooner I see him, the sooner it's over—the later I see him the fewer hours of absence left in the day. But no lover reflects.

Madeline. As you know, Colonel Erfurt, if you wish to make conversation I must listen.

Erfurt. Ah, you think I am wasting time! No, no—there is a purpose. It is true that I take an artistic pleasure in the beauty and vehemence of a passion, but as I study it I think always of the value it may have, not for me, but for the state.

Madeline. I understand you.

Erfurt. Excuse me. Lieutenant?
[*There is a scream off stage,* MADELINE *rises.*]

Schoen. Yes, sir?

Erfurt. I need the papers concerning Raoul St. Cloud. Will you bring them?

Schoen. At once.
[*There is another scream off stage.* SCHOEN *goes out.*]

Erfurt. Do you feel unreal here, Miss Guest?

Madeline. Yes, I do.

Erfurt. Do you know why?

Madeline. I'm not sure.

Erfurt. You will not offend me. No, I should like to hear.

Madeline. I have a horror of prisons. Of being shut up. And of those who shut people up.

Erfurt. But is that all? Surely it goes deeper?

Madeline. I once visited an asylum for the insane. Here—

Erfurt. Here it seems to you that the lunatics are in charge and those who are normal are restrained?

Madeline. Yes.

Erfurt. You see, I'm familiar with the notion. It recurs among those who come here for the first time. It's the natural and usual reaction. Because you have stopped, when you enter this room, from one world to another—from the old world to the new. You have stepped from freedom and chivalry and legend, into science, reality and control.

[SCHOEN *enters with the dossier.*]

Please—

[ERFURT *sits, examining the dossier.*]

Yes, I thought I remembered. M. St. Cloud is by way of being an amateur anthropologist?

Madeline. I believe so, yes.

Erfurt. He has found relief from the journalistic routine by examining the facial index and tracing the ancestry of mankind?

Madeline. Yes.

Erfurt. It would be easier if he had stuck to journalism.

Madeline. Why do you say so?

Erfurt. I have a review here of *Mein Kampf,* written by St. Cloud in 1931 for *Le Journal des Débats.* Unfortunately he analyzes our Fuehrer's theories somewhat to their disadvantage. He also takes occasion to comment on the Fuehrer's anatomical construction.

Madeline. This was printed in 1931?

Erfurt. Yes.

Madeline. And it is still held important?

Erfurt. Unfortunately again, there were recriminations in the press, and, to make matters worse, our leader was subjected to personal attack—which he remembers.

Madeline. Does this—have a bearing—on my request for an interview?

Erfurt. Miss Guest, this dossier carries a stamp, which might be interpreted: No Privileges. Now a visit from you would be regarded as a privilege, I'm certain.

Madeline. I may not see him?

Erfurt. I'm sorry, you may not see him.

Madeline. There was—a promise.

Erfurt. From whom?

Madeline. He refused his name. But he was a German official.

Erfurt. You should have insisted on the name. Would you accept such a commitment from a stranger?

Madeline. But he knew you. He has influence with you.

Erfurt. How do you know?

Madeline. It was he who arranged this appointment.

Erfurt. At a price?

Madeline. Yes.

Erfurt. There is a Latin adage—Caveat emptor.

Madeline. But if he was not a responsible official—how does it happen that he can arrange a meeting with you?

Erfurt. Ah, yes—I understand. There perhaps we should be willing to acknowledge a defect. State control is the only efficient control, but it requires a large corps of officials—a bureaucracy, if you like. Under a bureaucracy, there comes a time when the government mills grind slowly, and a modest amount of bribery becomes necessary to the functioning of the state.

Madeline. Then your government is for sale?

Erfurt. No, no, no—not at all. But the government, being wise, accepts this unavoidable bribery as a new form of taxation. Of whatever you paid the officer for the interview, he will keep only a part. The government will take its share. And thereby we convert a weakness into a source of strength. You are an American citizen, and therefore not taxable, yet we have collected a tax from you.

Madeline.
  [*Rising*]
It was promised me that I should see Raoul St. Cloud.

Erfurt. Going through the papers, I find that it cannot be arranged.

Madeline. I'm willing to pay for that, too.

Erfurt. You have misunderstood, Miss Guest. Not for a principality, not for half a kingdom, would any one of us run counter to a decision from Berlin.

Madeline. But I must see him. Do outsiders never visit the prisoners here?

Erfurt. Very seldom. The rules are against it. There are special cases.

Madeline. It happens somewhat at your discretion?

Erfurt. I interpret the rules, but the rules are not elastic, Miss Guest.

[*The inner door opens, and the* FLEURYS *are led through to the outer door. When she has passed through the inner wire door* MME. FLEURY *collapses and is carried out by a* GUARD. *What they have seen within has broken them down to speechless, whining animals. They can say nothing, hardly know where they are.* ERFURT *speaks in German to* SCHOEN.]

Verdammt nochmal, konnten Sie das nicht verhindern gerade wenn die Amerikanerin hier ist?

Schoen. Sie sagten fünfzehn Minuten, Herr Oberst.

Erfurt. I'm sorry about the interruption. Please sit down—

Madeline.

[*Facing him across his desk*]

Colonel Erfurt, I cannot accept what you have said as final. It's not easy to speak of love in this new world you have made—this wilderness of pain and lost children. I can't defend my love. I only know that since he was taken, I have had no hope save in the hope of his return, no rest from torment save in seeking him. Since I have known that he was here—the walls of the cruel and ugly prison have gone with me wherever I am. Since I have believed that there would come a moment when I would see him—I have loved only in the hope of that one point in time.

Erfurt. I believe you, Miss Guest. And I would help you if I could.

Madeline. Others go through that door.

Erfurt. No one will ever go through it to see Raoul St. Cloud. That is, and will remain, quite impossible. There is a terrible word written on these papers. The word *sterben.* It is not often used. I do not often see it. But when I do, I know that all decisions in that case are out of my hands.

Madeline. I cannot believe you, and I will not. These decisions are out of your hands only if you wish it so. You must let me see him—

Erfurt. It's impossible—

Madeline. Nothing's impossible! Perhaps I make a difficulty for you, perhaps it is easier to put me aside and go on with your work! But I will not be put aside! You shall not stop me! I shall haunt this prison! I shall appeal to your superiors! I shall not leave France till I have seen Raoul St. Cloud!

Erfurt. Shall I tell you what will happen if you stay in France?

Madeline. I know what must happen!

Erfurt. You will say to yourself, there must be a way out! There must be a weakness! There must be somewhere a corrupt guard! These hastily constructed camps cannot be impervious! You will go to work to find this one weakness you need, this little crevice which may widen to a crack in our system! You will use all the ardor and the ingenuity of a woman in love, and you will fail! Your love, your talent, your time and your money will be wasted! And now that you have heard this, now that you know this—will you be sensible? Will you give up this living dead man, and your dead love, and go sensibly back to America?

Madeline. No.

Erfurt. No? You are spoiled and soft, you Americans. You have never come up against sharp iron. It is your destiny to be beaten! Schoen, lassen Sie sie doch raus.

Madeline. I will never be beaten. Never. I will stay—and I will win!

Erfurt. If you are wise, you will go home now. Nobody wins here. This is a camp of dead men.

Madeline. I will stay, and I will win!
   [*She turns and goes out.*]

CURTAIN

CANDLE IN THE WIND

ACT TWO

Act Two

SCENE: The sitting room of MADELINE's *suite in the Plaza Athene in Paris. An inner door to the left, an outer door to the right. Curtained French windows in the center. A usual assortment of chairs, table and desk. It is September, 1941, one year later than Act One.* CISSIE *sits on couch at center, mending a stocking. A chair is wedged under the handle of the door. There is a knock, and* CISSIE *listens instead of moving. There is another knock.*

Maisie.
[*Off stage*]
Cissie!

Cissie.
[*Rising*]
I don't know you.

Maisie. Don't be an ass, Cissie. It's Maisie Tompkins.

Cissie. Who?

Maisie. It's big foot. You know, the American big foot.

Cissie. Yes, madame.
[*She removes the chair from under door handle and opens the door.* MAISIE *enters.*]

Maisie. Well, perhaps you wanted to be alone!
[CISSIE *replaces the chair under door handle.*]
You're an incredible ass, Cissie. That flying buttress is no good. It intimidates your friends, and arouses your enemies.

Cissie. It's very useful, madame.

Maisie. And don't call me madame! In spite of my height, size and reach, I'm still legally a maiden.
   [*She sits on the couch.*]

Cissie. Yes, mademoiselle.

Maisie. Is Miss Guest in?

Cissie. She goes all day to see German officials, but she will be here soon.

Maisie. Don't you know that if any German soldier wants to come in here he will?

Cissie. I have had experience with German soldiers.

Maisie. Where?

Cissie. First in Vienna, because I am Viennese. I was there when they took Austria. Then I was in Prague when they took Czecho-Slovakia. And I was here when they took France, bad luck. Always in hotels.

Maisie. And out of this wealth of experience, you learn to set chairs under door handles?

Cissie. Look, mademoiselle. A German soldier works by what is on his little card. He has orders on a little card. What to do with the proprietor, what to do with the guests. What to do when the door is open, what to do when the door is locked. But what to do when a chair is under the door, he does not have. Sometimes he goes away to find out.

Maisie. But he comes back.

Cissie. Then you have time. You can get the hell out!

Maisie. Where to?

Cissie. Maybe another hotel room.

Maisie. But sooner or later he catches up with you!
[*She goes to the window.*]

Cissie. Later, yes. But any time you have with no German soldier in your room, that is cake!

Maisie.
[*Looking out*]
I get you. They're goose-stepping again. About seven million of them. As far as the eye can see both ways. It gives me nausea.

Cissie. It's better not to look out!

Maisie. Where did you learn that wisdom?

Cissie. In Prague. One is tempted to drop things on them, and that's bad.

Maisie. Yes, I suppose it might lead to misunderstanding.

Cissie. Also maybe somebody next door drops something on them. Then they see you in the window and they shoot you!

Maisie.
[*Stepping back from the window*]
Yes, I see.

Cissie. And anyway, they want you to look at them. Why do they kick their feet so high? They think it's very attractive!

Maisie. Any luck with your marketing today?

Cissie. The usual luck.

Maisie. Well, I heard a rumor of meat at the new market, so I went over and stood in line. They offered me a quarter of cat meat. I don't mean meat for cats—no, part of the carcass of a slain cat. I wish now I'd bought it. I don't know what I had to go and get squeamish for, at the wrong moment. What do you mean by the usual luck?

Cissie. Turnips.

Maisie. Well, I was at the wrong counter, and didn't even get turnips this morning. You couldn't feed a third party—with an appetite like a diplodoccus?
[*She sits.*]

Cissie. Yes, we could.

Maisie. When you studied history was there a paragraph about the Parisians eating horse during the siege of 1870?

Cissie. Yes, mademoiselle, and the animals in the zoo.

Maisie. I used to be horrified! But by habit I'm a meat-eater, Cissie. It keeps running in mind—if I only had a horse. A whole horse to myself. It makes a lady shiver to think what she'd do if pressed! You're the next thing to a cannibal, Cissie!

Cissie. I?

Maisie. I'm on the verge of cannibalism, and you're very handy!

Cissie. No—no. I have two water crackers, that I was saving.
[*She opens a drawer of the desk, takes out a paper bag, and offers one cracker to* Maisie.]
May I offer you one?

Maisie. Bless you.
> [*Takes the cracker, bites into it*]

Is that a place for food?

Cissie. In the kitchen somebody might take them. The maid comes in to clean.

Maisie. You're not hungry?

Cissie. Everybody's always hungry.

Maisie. I had no breakfast—nor lunch—nor tiffin, nor tea. We've got to get out of this place, Cissie. Things are getting worse and worse.

Cissie. Isn't Miss Guest going back to America, mademoiselle?

Maisie. She says she is, but then she puts it off from week to week.

Cissie. I came to work for her because she was American. She promised to take me with her.

Maisie.
> [*She has finished the cracker and starts picking up crumbs from her lap and eating them.*]

Well, I've been sitting around this modern version of hell long enough now, waiting for her to give up and go back with me. But she's a monomaniac now. It's really an obsession with her. She won't give up, and she won't go.

Cissie. If she waits for the officer in the prison camp, then perhaps we stay a long time in France.

Maisie. Yes. Tell me, did you ever know anybody to escape? Does it happen?

Cissie. Yes, once. It was somebody I wished him to stay where he was. That kind could escape.

Maisie. But the one you want? The one you'd move heaven and earth to get out?

Cissie. I should say never.

Maisie. Yes, I should say never. That's what she won't believe.
[*There is a knock at the outer door.* Cissie *puts her finger to her lips. There is another knock, then the door handle moves. A pause.*]

Cissie.
[*Whispering*]
You see, he goes away.

Maisie.
[*Rising, crossing to the door*]
Well I'm not going to be found here when he gets back!
[*She opens the door.*]
Yes! Yes! You wanted something?

Mueller.
[*Outside*]
I wished to find Miss Guest.

Maisie. She's not in.

Mueller. Thank you. Could you tell me when she is expected to return?

Maisie. Within a few minutes, I think.

Cissie. Yes, she should be here by now.

Mueller. Thank you. I'm sorry to trouble you.

Maisie. You're quite welcome.
  [*She closes the door.*]
  Only I wish you'd explain why you come trying people's doors, my mannie.
  [*To* CISSIE]
  Did you recognize that uniform?

Cissie. No. He's not a soldier.

Maisie. Perhaps one of Himmler's boys.

Cissie. It could be.
  [CISSIE *replaces the chair under the handle of the door.*]

Maisie. It's getting too thick around here for comfort. What kind of devious business are we in now? I wonder—

Cissie. Yes.

Maisie. I won't stay any longer. And I shall make that very clear. Today. By the way Cissie, don't worry too much about getting out of France. If we can't get a passport fixed up for you, the fishermen are still carrying passengers from Brittany to England.

Cissie. Oh, thank you mademoiselle.
  [*There is a knock on the outside door again.*]
  It's Miss Guest.
  [*She removes the chair from under the handle, and opens the door.* MADELINE *enters.* CISSIE *closes the door after her.*]

Madeline. Thank you Cissie. Oh, Maisie, I hoped you'd be here.

Maisie. I wish you lived on another street. Somewhere in the East Seventies.

Cissie. There was a man just now to see you.

Madeline. Oh?

Cissie. Not a soldier, but with a uniform.

Madeline. Oh, I must have passed him. But it doesn't matter. He'll be back, I think.

Maisie. I think perhaps I'll be leaving.

Madeline. Oh no, Maisie. It's not an official visit.

Maisie. He did try the door handle.

Madeline. He did? Well, I'm beyond objecting to that. Is there anything for the inner woman, Cissie? Any slight thing?

Cissie. I'm afraid—

Madeline. Any tea?

Cissie. Birch bark tea.

Madeline. That's all right—and just a trace of—

Cissie. There's a water cracker.
[*She holds out the paper bag to* MADELINE.]

Madeline. That's your water cracker, Cissie. I won't take that.

Cissie. There's nothing else except the turnips, and they're for dinner. If you would share the water cracker with me?

Maisie. Personally I had a whole one.

Madeline. That's immoral. Yes, I will share it with you, Cissie.

Cissie. I'll get the tea.
  [*She goes within.*]

Maisie. You look tired.

Madeline.
  [*Lying back on the couch*]
  No, not tired. Just shabby, and down at heel, and completely out of cold cream.

Maisie. Tired too. And hungry.

Madeline. Not beyond bearing.

Maisie. You've been going it like a soldier for a whole year, Madeline. And whether you'll admit it or not you're tired and hungry, and just about done in. I can remember four distinct plots to get Raoul out of that camp. Four times you've built up a fantastic and elaborate machine—complete with corrupt guards, escape, transportation, fake passport, underground passage out of occupied France, and God knows what all, and then it always crashed because somebody squealed and he couldn't get out of the camp after all. It's about to happen again—I can see that same feverish hope in your eyes that's been there so often before. And it won't work, and then you'll be in despair again.

Madeline. This time—we have a chance.

Maisie. It's come to that now. This time you have a chance. You used to be sure, remember?

Madeline. Maisie, the chance was never so good before. Never once. There are three guards on the inside, helping. Because I've promised to get them to America if things turn out well.

Maisie. You believe they're helping?

Madeline. Yes.

Maisie. You've believed it before.

Madeline. Oh, Maisie—they torture people there—and they die under it. Suppose we came a day late. And then suppose we came just in time, when they were about—to kill him. I want to come in time, Maisie.

Maisie. I know, Madeline—that's why I stayed with you—

Madeline. You were wonderful to stay. I couldn't have kept on without you.

Maisie. And yet we have to look at things as they are. I came to the end of my money a good while ago, and you helped me out. But that can't go on forever.—Even you—

Madeline. No. I'm nearly at the end.

Maisie. Wouldn't it be wise if you were to turn over to me what we'll need to get out of France and to America, we three?

Madeline. Yes. I'll do that. I've been going over what I have. Would three thousand take us home?

Maisie. I think so, with a little to spare.

Madeline. But with bribes, we might need it?

Maisie. Yes.

Madeline. You shall have it tomorrow.—Only—

Maisie. Yes?

Madeline. That means that—with what I'm spending tonight—that's all we'll have.

Maisie. You see, if we're caught here without money, then it's completely hopeless. If we get out—you might earn enough to come back and try again.—

Madeline. Yes, I've thought of that—

Maisie. Then we're agreed?

Madeline. Yes.
[*She rises and embraces* Maisie, *as* Cissie *enters with the tea tray.*]
Oh, thank you, Cissie. Shall I break it?
[*She picks up the one remaining cracker.*]

Cissie. Please.

Maisie. No, no, not three parts.
[Cissie *goes within again.*]

Madeline. Don't be silly. You're having tea with us.

Maisie. I'm weak; I accept.
[*There is a knock at the outer door.* Madeline *rises, puts tea tray down on the desk, and opens the door.*]

Madeline. Come in.
[Corporal Mueller *stands just outside the door.*]
Come in.
[Mueller *enters.*]
You wish to see me alone, of course.

Mueller. I could return, perhaps?

Madeline. No, no—
  [*To* MAISIE]
  If you don't mind, Maisie—

Maisie. Not at all.
  [*Starts to go toward the bedroom*]

Mueller. I would rather there was no one in the apartment.

Maisie. Shall I wait in the hall?

Mueller. Please.
  [MAISIE *crosses to the desk, picks up her cup and saucer, and goes out by the hall.* MUELLER *closes the door after her.*]

Madeline. You didn't come to the Tabarin.

Mueller. I was being followed. This afternoon they lost me, so I came here.

Madeline. You're distrusted?

Mueller. I think not. They have us watched from time to time, just to make sure.

Madeline. You promised to bring a note from M. St. Cloud.

Mueller. Here it is. Forgive me—
  [*He starts to look about, opens the bedroom door.*]

Cissie.
  [*Outside*]
  Was wollen Sie?
  [*She comes in.*]
  Mademoiselle—

· 60 ·

Madeline. Oh, Cissie—I forgot—

[CISSIE *goes out to the hall.* MUELLER *shuts the door.*]

Now I must know all the plans in detail.

Mueller. What do you want me to tell you?

Madeline. I have a slight anxiety—please sit down—

[MUELLER *sits.*]

about a daylight escape. Why must it happen in the afternoon?

Mueller. Is it necessary for you to know this?

Madeline. Before I give you any money, it is necessary that I know everything.

Mueller. It must be at three tomorrow because we take advantage of something which will happen at the camp tomorrow at that hour.—

Madeline. What will happen?

Mueller. Sometimes the state wishes prisoners to be free, but cannot dismiss them publicly. Tomorrow it is arranged that certain prisoners depart under fire.

Madeline. And how do you know this?

Mueller. I am one of the guards ordered to assist.

Madeline. Tell me how it will be done. Do you mean—in the confusion—M. St. Cloud will somehow slip out of the enclosure with the others?

Mueller. Something like that. The fence is being repaired at one point. Guards and prisoners go back and forth through the opening. Now at exactly three o'clock, an automobile will be drawn up across the road, and certain prisoners are instructed to jump into the car, which will drive away. The guards will fire over the car. M. St. Cloud will be among the prisoners chosen for the work at the bridge, and he will slip into the car also. The driver is a friend of mine. He will take M. St. Cloud to the room you have specified in the Bordeaux Apartments.

Madeline. And the men for whom the escape was planned?

Mueller. I will tell them at the last moment that another is to join them.

Madeline. And the guards who are helping you? You are sure of each of them? They are all ready and willing to go through with this?

Mueller. Don't worry; they will carry out their part.

Madeline. And you have made my appointment with Colonel Erfurt for three?

Mueller. Yes, there is an appointment made for you with Colonel Erfurt for three o'clock. We count on you to keep him at his desk with a discussion of the prison rules.

Madeline. Have you brought the book?

Mueller. Yes, and I have marked the page. It would be better if you could be there a little before three, just to keep him in his office.

Madeline. I shall keep him there if I can. As long as I can. I have placed half the money in this one envelope, as I promised. The other half I will give to the driver of the car when he comes to the apartment.

Mueller. I will have to have that now.

Madeline. That was not our bargain.

Mueller. The others refuse to take part unless I can put the money in their hands tonight. You see, after the break, we must all three leave France instantly. We have no wish to die here.

Madeline. Very well.
> [*She hands him another envelope.*]

Mueller. If there is anything else I can do? You haven't asked about passports.

Madeline. I've arranged that separately.

Mueller. Good. Good-bye.

Madeline. Good-bye. And thanks from my heart for this.

Mueller. Thank you. But it is not a matter of sentiment.
> [*He clicks his heels, opens the door and goes out.* MADELINE *stands looking at the letter from* RAOUL. *The door opens again, and* MAISIE *and* CISSIE *enter.*]

Maisie. Does it go well?

Madeline. I have a note from him. In his own hand. No one could write like that. This time it comes true.
> [*She kisses* MAISIE.]

Tomorrow at three—something will happen!

Maisie. In broad daylight?

Madeline. Yes.

Maisie. It sounds unlikely again.

Madeline. We must choose what we'll take, Cissie, and be ready to go tomorrow.

Cissie. Yes, mademoiselle.
[*She goes out.*]

Maisie. That passport factory wants an enormous sum for Cissie's visa.

Madeline. Please don't quarrel with them over money, Maisie. There mustn't be any delay; we're leaving in the afternoon.

Maisie. You and I go by plane?

Madeline. I suppose so.

Maisie. And Raoul by underground?

Madeline. Yes. Underground to the coast, then with a fisherman to England.

Maisie. Will he be safe?

Madeline. Safe? No, not safe, but cared for and watched over. When a prisoner escapes, the whole French nation hides him, helps him, sends him on his way. All those that help him will put themselves in danger of death—but they'll help him. The peasants and shop-keepers that give him shelter and food and pass him through the lines are all likely to be shot the next morning, but they'll help him anyway. How could anybody give up when there's courage like that around us? There are such gallant, such wonderful people in the world! They make one believe in so many things, that England will win, that France will be free, and that he will be free tomorrow! Only, Maisie?—

Maisie. Yes, darling—

Madeline. It's been a year, and I begin to find so much

gray in my hair. When I look in the mirror, there are deep lines in my face that he never saw. Will he turn away from me, Maisie?

Maisie. Nonsense. There'll be plenty of gray in his hair, and lines in his face.

Madeline. One thing I know now. I went into this love easily, lightly even, but I shall never see beyond it while I live.

CURTAIN

Act Two

SCENE: *The office of the Concentration Camp again.*
LIEUTENANT SCHOEN *sits at his desk.* ERFURT'S *place is
empty, but a* GUARD *stands as usual at the door at the
right.* CORPORAL BEHRENS *looks in through grating.*

Behrens. Ist der Alte hier?

Guard. Nein.
[*He opens the door, admitting* BEHRENS *and* CORPORAL
SCHULTZ.]

Behrens. Lieutenant?

Schoen. Yes.

Behrens. Got a cigarette?

Schoen. The Commandant is due here any minute.

Behrens. We have a tough job, and my comrade gets a
little sick. Let him sit here and have a smoke.
[SCHOEN *gives* SCHULTZ *a cigarette.*]

Schultz. Thanks, that's better.

Behrens. He don't like it in there any more; he goes green
around the edges.

Schultz. You lie, I do like it! A man can ask for a
cigarette.

Behrens. Your face was green, buebchen.

Schultz. You lie! I like it well enough. At first I didn't;
at first it made me sick. But now I find there's a kind

of—yes, there's a kind of joy in it—a kind of joy in the workmanship—it's a thing you do for the state, and therefore you do it well.

Behrens. Tell him what we did this afternoon.

Schultz. This afternoon, yes. A funny thing we did this afternoon—we took one of them—

Schoen. I don't care to hear it! You will sit quietly, or go back inside.

Schultz. Yes, Lieutenant.

Erfurt.
   [*Off stage*]
Nein—auf keinen Fall—
   [BEHRENS *and* SCHULTZ *hurry to the inner door, as* ERFURT *enters, and go out with hasty salutes.*]
What are they doing here?

Schoen. Should I be stricter with the guards, Colonel Erfurt?

Erfurt. When you keep bloodhounds, you must let them run. Once take the pride out of them, and they will never again sink their teeth with the same gusto.

Schoen. Good. I'll take my cue from that.

Erfurt. I've sometimes wondered if you were set here to watch me.

Schoen. I hope I have not deserved that imputation. Why do you say this?

Erfurt. I'm wondering why I said it. One can't always say what's expected of him.

Schoen. Have I displeased you in some way, sir?

Erfurt. Whether we like it or not, there's a barrier between those who were men when our Fuehrer came to power and those who were children.

Schoen. But not between us, I assure you.

Erfurt. Have you never looked at men of my generation, thinking: They are not pure? They have lived under a loose, degenerate regime—they may long for it again—may prove untrue to the spartan thought and ascetic way of life that must prevail if we are to win?

Schoen. This has occurred to me, yes, but then I have remembered that our great leaders are among the older men, our greatest leaders.

Erfurt. And so that doubt is cancelled?

Schoen. It is cancelled. However I have reflected on National Socialism, Colonel Erfurt, and it seems to me that I observe something.

Erfurt. What is it?

Schoen. It seems to be the heart of our system that no man works alone. We hunt in pairs, or run in packs. One man alone is dangerous.

Erfurt. You mean to say that no man is given complete responsibility?

Schoen. I have not said that. I have said that two men together are found more dependable than one alone.

Erfurt. It could be said then that we watch each other?

Schoen. You are my superior officer, Colonel Erfurt. It

is your duty to watch me, no doubt. As for myself, I am placed here under orders.

Erfurt. Then why do you make each week a supplementary report to Berlin?

   [*Pause*]

You do make such a report?

   [*Pause*]

Out of the kindness of your heart? You might at least have told me.

Schoen. I was directed not to tell you.

Erfurt. Of course. I should have known. I am irritable today. You will kindly overlook my rudeness.

Schoen. Surely.

   [*He looks at his watch.*]

It's five minutes to three. Should I admit Miss Guest now?

Erfurt. Oh, Miss Guest—

   [*Looks at his watch*]

Yes, let her come in.

   [SCHOEN *pushes a buzzer and a* GUARD *appears.*]

Schoen. Bringen Sie Miss Guest herein.

Guard. Jawohl, Herr Lieutenant.

   [*He ushers* MADELINE *in.*]

Erfurt.

   [*Rising*]

Come in, Miss Guest. This must be a short interview, for I have much to do. Please sit down.

Madeline.

    [*Seating herself*]

I shall make it brief, Colonel Erfurt. There are two things of which I wish to speak.

Erfurt. Come then.

Madeline. First, I shall not be able to remain much longer in France.

Erfurt. Yes, I know.

Madeline. Before I leave—

Erfurt. You are anxious to interview a certain prisoner?

Madeline. Yes.

Erfurt. The situation is unchanged.

Madeline. Second, I have been allowed to read a copy of the book of orders issued to the directors of prisons by the authorities of the Third Reich. In the third section, page 57, it is distinctly stated that you may grant interviews with inmates at will.

Erfurt.

    [*Picking up a small book from his desk*]

Is this the volume?

Madeline.

    [*Looking at the book*]

Yes.

Erfurt. It is forbidden to laymen; however you are quite right.

    [*Turning pages*]

Page 57. Only you should have read further. I have

the power to allow interviews without check, but I am responsible to my superiors for any abuse of that power.

[*Starts to close book*]

Madeline. May I see the paragraph?

Erfurt. Please.

[*He hands her the book.*]

Madeline. And how is abuse of that power defined.

Erfurt. It is not defined; that's the point. Each man is held responsible for the results of his actions.

Madeline. I have had legal advice concerning your responsibility, Colonel Erfurt, and, unless I have misunderstood, the commandants of camps or prisons are given wide latitude in the treatment of inmates.

Erfurt. Miss Guest, for a little fee you can obtain any version of our laws you wish—

Madeline. There are political prisoners under your supervision—who live in their own homes—who—

[GUARD *enters from the left.*]

Erfurt. Excuse me—

[*To the* GUARD]

Was giebst?

Guard. Corporal Mueller.

Erfurt. Herein mit ihm.

[*The* GUARD *exits as* MUELLER *enters.*]

Mueller. Herr Oberst, Sie haben befohlen sie zu erinnern.

[*He lays a report on* ERFURT's *desk.* ERFURT *stamps a pass for him, and he goes inside.*]

· 71 ·

Madeline. Is M. St. Cloud still here?

Erfurt. Yes.

Madeline. Is he well?

Erfurt. Yes, he is in excellent health. Partly as a consequence, I may tell you now, of your continued interest in him.

Madeline. Mine?

Erfurt. Yes. We had no doubt that you were in touch with friends in your own country. We thought it to our advantage that you should not be able to report ill treatment in this instance. Also, while he lived, and you were well to do, you sent tribute to Berlin.

Madeline. Yes, I see.

Erfurt. However, the attitude of your government is now so definitely hostile, that we have nothing more to gain by leniency, and we note each withdrawal from your account. You understand?

[*The clock strikes three.*]

Madeline. Yes.

[*There is a pause, then a machine-gun begins to bark in the distance. A siren and a bell are heard simultaneously.* MADELINE *rises.* SCHOEN *also rises and opens the gate for a* GUARD *who passes through rapidly to the inner door. As the siren dies away* SCHOEN's *telephone rings.* SCHOEN *picks it up and listens.*]

Schoen. Alles in Ordnung.

Erfurt. Don't be disturbed. This is not an alert. Once in a while we allow some prisoners to escape. We blow the siren and do a great deal of shooting and running about, and certain prisoners drive away in a car, but we want them to go. It is all prearranged. It's a political matter.

Madeline. How happy they must be to leave this place.
[*She rises.*]
I fear there is nothing to be gained by prolonging this interview, Colonel Erfurt. This will be my last visit here.
[*She turns to go.*]

Erfurt. You are leaving?

Madeline. I—yes—you gave me my answer long ago—nothing that I can say to you brings me nearer to him. I'll go now.
[*She lifts a hand to the gate.*]
Please—

Erfurt. Not yet. You have kept a long and bitter vigil here in France, I know. Even I am not insensible to that. There is a character in Shakespeare who says—"Some good I mean to do, despite of mine own nature." Well, I shall take a leaf from Shakespeare. Let them bring in St. Cloud!

Schoen.
[*Rising*]
Yes, sir.

Madeline.
[*Quickly, to* SCHOEN]
No, not now.

Erfurt. Not now? Did I hear correctly? You do not wish to see M. St. Cloud?

· 73 ·

Madeline. Let me come tomorrow.

Erfurt. Why tomorrow?

Madeline.

    [*Leaning against the cage*]

It would be better. I hadn't expected that you would say this. You've made it so difficult, and now suddenly —I've waited so long—I'm afraid I'll be ill—please let me come tomorrow.

Erfurt. Not tomorrow, today. Have them bring in St. Cloud at once!

Schoen.

    [*Into telephone*]

Offizier, St. Cloud vorführen.

    [*Hangs up phone*]

Erfurt. When I read Shakespeare nowadays, I come to the reluctant conclusion that he is essentially alien to us. He makes, for instance—Edmund the villain in Lear.

    [SCHOEN *looks at* MADELINE, *sees her sway—rises—takes a glass of water from his desk and offers it to her. She shakes her head. He returns with the glass to his desk, and sits.*]

And what is Edmund? A Machiavellian, a clever young fellow with no illusions, and only those scruples proper to a sensible young man. But Shakespeare makes him the villain of the piece, and kills him off in miserable fashion. No, Shakespeare's got the whole moral system upside down. In real life the strong and ruthless win, and the weak suffer. And that's how it should be, or must be.

    [*The right hand door opens, admitting* RAOUL *and a*

GUARD. MADELINE *and* RAOUL *look at each other for a moment.*]

Madeline. Oh, God.

[*She bows her head, and starts to cry quietly. There is a pause.*]

Erfurt. You weren't expecting this, I know. You thought him elsewhere. Now I could have arranged that too, only it would have meant the end of my career, very definitely. An ordinary escape might be forgiven, but M. St. Cloud I must keep safe, or step down into the ranks. Therefore I keep him safe. Perhaps I should warn you now to look well at each other, for this may be your last meeting.

Madeline. Raoul.

Raoul. Yes Madeline.

Madeline.

[*Crossing to him*]
You know—how hard I've tried?

Raoul. Yes, I know.

Madeline. We've been betrayed, I think.

Raoul. Yes, many times. And again today. You must leave France and take up your life. You've wasted too much time on the impossible.

Madeline. Are you in pain, Raoul? You moved as if you were in pain.

Raoul. No, no. We're well treated here. Don't worry about that.

Madeline.

[*Moving a step closer to him*]
Could I kiss you?

Raoul. No, not here. It's enough to see you. That's what I prayed for.

Madeline. You received my messages?

Raoul. No, they allow no messages. But sometimes a whisper comes through the walls. I've known where you were. Sometimes I've even known what you did. In a strange way I've walked with you daily.

Madeline. And I with you.

Raoul. Remembering you, and the days we had together. When it was ugliest here, the days and nights were filled with words from you to me.

Madeline. I know.

Erfurt.
[*After a pause*]
If you have no more to say, perhaps we may go on to other matters. Is that all?

Raoul. You must not think we've lost! Even though we should lose, we have won! They know what they are, and no words can cover it!

Madeline. We've not lost yet! Never believe I'd say we've lost!

Erfurt. Take him back to his cell.
[*They lead* RAOUL *out.*]
You are dismissed.
[MADELINE *turns on him.*]
And don't say that you'll strike me, or that you'll die,

· 76 ·

for I speak from long experience, and you'll do neither.
You'll go home again, for the last time.

Madeline. Yes.

Erfurt. You are dismissed.

> [MADELINE *goes to the gate.* SCHOEN *sits watching her,
> not moving.*]

Schoen!—

> [SCHOEN *rises and opens the gate.* MADELINE *goes slowly
> out.* SCHOEN *closes the gate and looks out after her.*]

And yet something perishes with them when they are
exterminated. A kind of decadent beauty one hates to
lose.

CURTAIN

Act Two

SCENE: The sitting room in the hotel again. MAISIE *is sitting at desk addressing tags.* CISSIE *sits on the couch, tying a tag on a small leather case. Several suitcases are lying on the floor, ready for the journey. Early evening of the same day.*

Cissie. If I get the visa, mademoiselle, then I won't need the passage on the fisherman's boat.

Maisie. Well, it won't be wasted. There's always somebody waiting to get out.

Cissie. Mademoiselle, is it true you can buy fruit and cheese and butter on the streets in New York? All you want?

Maisie. Yes.

Cissie. From open wagons on the streets?

Maisie. Yes.

Cissie. Could one person buy all that was on the wagon?

Maisie. If he wanted to.

Cissie. Have you seen this yourself?

Maisie. Oh, yes.

Cissie. Have you ever bought all that was on a wagon?

Maisie. Well, in my time I've made a terrible consumption of butterfats and cheese, but never by the wagon-load.

Cissie. I think if I ever saw it I'd buy a whole wagon-load, and take it home. I shall never stop being hungry.

Maisie. You'll find that you can't eat much at a time. Woman wants but little food and drink, she just wants that little fairly regular.

Cissie. Of course, for me, America is only a dream.

Maisie. I used to walk around on it, so it must be solid.

Cissie. It may be that you walked in a dream. I myself have walked there in a dream. They say when you dream in English, then you are no longer German, then you can be an American.

Maisie. There may be something in that.

Cissie. I dreamed once that I walked among the food wagons, and spoke English—spoke it clearly—and asked for ice cream. And the man filled a great vase with ice cream, and it piled up and up and up—like a white cloud, and when I reached for it, it blew away. I woke up, and now I'm always hungry, and I cannot dream in English again.

Maisie. It'll come back.

Cissie. Mademoiselle?

Maisie. Yes.

Cissie. I wonder if they would ever arrest an American lady?

Maisie. What makes you say that?

Cissie. It's after four o'clock, and she hasn't come.

Maisie. They sometimes arrest Americans, but they don't keep them long. They're very careful about Americans.

Cissie. But when she tries and tries to get him out of the camp, isn't that—

Maisie. High treason? It certainly is. It's high treason in this country to steal a cake of soap—it's high treason to think Hitler walks like a woman, but he does. We're all guilty of that.

Cissie. Yes, I suppose.
[*The right-hand door opens.* MADELINE *enters.* CISSIE *rises.*]
Oh, no—we don't go?

Madeline. I don't.

Maisie. What happened?

Madeline. It was as you predicted. He's still in the camp. I saw him.

Maisie. He's well?

Madeline. He says so.

Maisie. There's nothing to do?

Madeline. I don't know, not at the moment.

Maisie.
[*Rising*]
Sit down, darling. You look ready to collapse.

Madeline. I'm not tired.

Maisie.
[*Going to her*]
But sit down anyway. Is this the end of our string?

Madeline. Unpack my bags, Cissie.
[CISSIE *picks up the bags, and goes into the bedroom, closing door after her.*]

· 80 ·

I've been trying to think, but I can't think yet. He'd been beaten. I could see it.

Maisie. I hate to say this, Madeline, but it's hard fact, and we must face it. They'll never let go of Raoul.

Madeline. They must, Maisie.

Maisie. And you must go now. Don't have the bags unpacked. You can't help Raoul without money; you can't even live. There's another cable from California today. They're still offering you a fortune.

Madeline. I feel that if I let go, just once, for a day—it might be deadly to him.

Maisie. But the sooner you're home, the sooner you can return, the sooner you can help.

Madeline. Maybe. Yes I suppose so. We'd better try it. [*She sits wearily.*]

Maisie. I think we should.

Madeline. And yet, what if—I couldn't return? Isn't that possible?

Maisie. Yes. You'd have to face that.

Madeline. And what if—I couldn't return, and couldn't save him—and had to try to forget? Isn't that possible?

Maisie. Yes.

Madeline. What if I did forget, Maisie? Because I had to?

Maisie. I just think going is your only chance.

Madeline. You don't say his only chance.

Maisie. Yes, his only chance too.

Madeline. Yes, perhaps—

[*There is a knock on the outer door.* Maisie *opens it.* Lieutenant Schoen *is standing in the doorway.*]

Schoen.

I'm Lieutenant Schoen. I wish to see Miss Guest.

Madeline. Yes, come in.

[Schoen *enters.* Maisie *closes door, and stands below it.*]

Schoen. You remember me, Miss Guest? I'm from the prison.

Madeline. Yes, I remember. You have a message for me?

Schoen. No. I wish to see you concerning a personal matter if I can.

Madeline. What is it?

Schoen. If you will permit me, it would be easier to speak if we were alone.

Madeline. What personal matter do you mean?

Schoen. It would be easier—

Maisie. Shall I leave you with him, Madeline?

Madeline. Not yet. Do you wish to see me about Raoul St. Cloud?

Schoen. I would rather say nothing.

Madeline. Miss Tompkins is an American, as I am, and an old friend. She stayed in Paris to help me, if she could—to help secure the release of M. St. Cloud. If you have any honest business with me, you may speak it out quite frankly before her.

Schoen. Is there a telephone in this room?

Madeline.

[*Indicating the phone*]

It is not attached, and we have insulated the outlet with books.

Schoen. Yes.

Madeline. If you cannot speak while Miss Tompkins is in the room, I'll ask her to leave. But frankly I should prefer that she be present.

Schoen. Yes. I will say what I came to say. I have seen you, as you know, many times in Direktor Erfurt's office. I have also seen M. St. Cloud there. I feel that I know you both well, for I have listened carefully, and you are not ordinary people.

Madeline. Thank you.

Schoen. You have seen me only with your enemies, and so you think of me as an enemy, yet perhaps I can help you.

Madeline. In what way?

Schoen. To set your friend free.

Madeline. You are offering to help me—to help M. St. Cloud escape from the camp?

Schoen. I think I can advise you concerning it.

Madeline. Do you expect me to trust you?

Schoen. Yes, I see. Others have come too, offering to help, and you have trusted them—to no purpose.

Madeline. Unless I am mistaken they came to me, one and all, from your superior officer, Colonel Erfurt, for one and all they betrayed me to him.

Schoen. Forgive me if I place the matter on a realistic basis. You know who I am. In the Third Reich, and in our service, there is little money, as you know. I have at the moment, a desperate need of money. Perhaps you will forgive me if I do not go into the reason, but money I must have.

Madeline. I have no more money.

Schoen. Can you say that when you wear such a ring on your finger?

Madeline. I can't sell that.

Schoen. It came from him, perhaps? Could there be a more fitting use for his gift?

Madeline. You say you need money, but money won't be much good to you if you are caught aiding an escape!

Schoen. My need is such that I have not looked beyond it. I will somehow cover what I do.

Madeline. What plan have you in mind?

Schoen. Erfurt goes to Berlin tomorrow. I shall be in charge of the camp for some days. I should place M. St. Cloud in solitary confinement, and place with him the tools wherewith to free himself. There is a defect in our solitary system, and it has several times occurred to me that I would know how to escape from it.

Madeline. You could dispose of the diamond?

Schoen. Yes, easily.

Madeline. And it would bring enough to cover necessary expenses?

Schoen. I would think so, even in the present market.

Madeline. It always comes to this in the end. A certain amount of money, a plausible plan of escape. But something always goes wrong.

Schoen. How could I prove to you that I am not like the others?

Madeline. Could it be proved?

Schoen. I have glimpsed something in you—and in M. St. Cloud—that I admire. I do honestly wish that M. St. Cloud might have his liberty.

Madeline.
[*Going to* MAISIE, *taking her hand*]
Maisie—Maisie!—

Maisie. What position does this officer occupy at the camp?

Madeline. I've seen him always in Colonel Erfurt's office.

Maisie. Are you the Director's secretary?

Schoen. His assistant.

Maisie. The game grows fairly obvious, Madeline. They've run out of messengers. They think you may have saved a few dollars—no doubt they've noticed the diamond on your finger, but they can't find a new face in their Gestapo to collect from you. The Director looks round him, and here's his old stand-by, Lieutenant Schoen, as reliable as they come. "We'll send Schoen," he says. "But she knows Schoen, she's seen him a dozen times!" "Never mind, tell a big enough lie, and it's always believed." That's out of the horse's mouth. You don't know how to dramatize your story, Lieutenant. I've heard several of Erfurt's little prattlers, and you're easily in last place.

Madeline. I have tried to believe you, Lieutenant Schoen. The others I have believed—enough to employ them. But I have heard the story too often. It no longer convinces me.

Schoen. I'm sorry. I have never been a good salesman. I'm truly sorry. And I cannot give up so easily. Perhaps you will think better of it later this evening. When you are alone. It must be this evening, or not at all. Let me leave a telephone number.

[*Goes to the desk, writes a number on the pad*]

I can be reached at this number at any time before six.

Maisie. Would an honest man dare to leave his telephone number about? Certainly not!

Madeline. I shall not deal further with Colonel Erfurt or his agents.

Schoen. You believe me his agent?

Madeline. Yes.

Schoen. You are right, Miss Guest. I was sent by Erfurt; believe none of us.

Madeline. Thank you.

Schoen. I speak the truth when I say that I wish you well.

Madeline. Thank you.

Schoen. Good night.

Madeline. Good night.

[*He bows and goes out.*]

Maisie. He wasn't lying about who sent him. That was gospel. And so ends that chapter. You can't bribe anybody on the inside of the camp. It just doesn't work.

Madeline. Is there any other way to go to work?

Maisie. I haven't been able to think of any. Should we try to arrange about Cissie's visa now?

Madeline. I suppose so.

Maisie. Cissie—we're going!

Cissie.
   [*Entering*]
   Yes, mademoiselle.

Madeline. Would you mind—if I stayed here? They know you, these people. They'll do what they can.

Maisie. Are you sure you want to be here alone?

Madeline. I'm sure I don't want to go out, and face people.

Maisie. Wouldn't it be good for you, though?

Madeline. No darling, truly.

Maisie. Cissie and I will go then. Come, Cissie—

Madeline. I wish you luck with everything, Cissie.

Cissie. Yes, thank you, I know.

Maisie. There's only one thing—a girl has to go on, has to. No matter what happens.

Madeline. Yes, no matter.

Maisie. We'll come back as soon as we can.

Madeline. Right.

[MAISIE *and* CISSIE *go out, closing the door.* MADELINE *opens her bag, takes out a mirror and stares at her reflection for a moment.*]

Yes, Madeline—you must learn to live without Raoul. If there's to be no Raoul, you must learn to live without him. He would forgive your gray hairs, for his own is graying now. He would forgive those crow-tracks around your eyes, for the crows have torn at him too. But nobody else would forgive you, Madeline. The crowds won't forgive. They will say that you are old. Raoul would forgive you, Madeline, but there is no Raoul. Wipe out these lines, and weep less in these sleepless nights, for you must go forward without him. That is your lesson, Madeline. Learn it by heart, and never forget.

I can't, I can't—I can't.

[*She picks up the telephone slip from desk.*]

Passy 6340—

CURTAIN

Act Two

SCENE: The same, except that the velvet drapes at the windows have been drawn, and the books have been removed from the telephone outlet. MADELINE is standing, looking out window as curtain rises. There is a knock on the outer door.

Madeline. Come in.

[SCHOEN *enters, closing the door behind him.*]

Schoen. You asked me to come.

Madeline. You said something before you left, as you stood in the doorway; that you wished us well, that I should trust none of you.

Schoen. Yes.

Madeline. But now I know I can trust you.

Schoen. You can trust nobody.

Madeline. You told me that you came to betray me. You spoke the first honest word I have ever heard across the barrier that shuts you all in from the world. Perhaps you didn't intend it, but you became my friend with that word.

Schoen. I fear there is nothing to gain by further discussion.

Madeline. Why did you speak the truth to me?

Schoen. I have been sorry for you for many months. And for M. St. Cloud. One must look on at many things—

but there comes a time when one wishes to put the victim out of his misery. It's not a crime, even in the Reich, to feel sympathy with suffering.

Madeline. But to help, that's a crime?

Schoen. Even in your own country, it is a crime to aid a criminal.

Madeline. Have you thought what it would be like to live in another country? Where there is freedom of thought, where the state allows all possible freedom?

Schoen. I have thought of it. You must remember that we regard that as a diseased condition.

Madeline. Yet you have thought of it.

Schoen. Yes.

Madeline. Then you must have wished for freedom.

Schoen. Why must I?

Madeline. I have been thinking of these things too.

Schoen. Then tell me why?

Madeline. Because no wild thing was ever shut in a cage without wishing for freedom. And of all wild things in the world, the most uncontrollable—the least tameable— is the human mind. No king or priest or dictator has ever tamed it. It cannot rest in captivity. It cannot sleep. It has no relish for prison food. And the mind of Germany is caged.

Schoen. Caged by our enemies.

Madeline. Do you believe that?
   [SCHOEN *looks nervously about the room.*]

No. You are free here. In this room there is no compulsion on you to lie.

Schoen. This is not a useful conversation.

Madeline. I have seen many men in the world you live in who hate that world. There is a certain veiled regard in the eyes of those who must forever dissemble their unrest, who never dare speak out. And of all those who carry this look about with them, you have seemed the most unhappy. From the first day I saw you in Erfurt's office that look has been on your face. I didn't know what it meant then, but I know now.

Schoen. You will forgive me, but I must go.
[*He turns, and crosses to the door.*]

Madeline. I wish you to take this ring—the one you asked for this afternoon.
[*She offers the ring.*]

Schoen. Why do you offer it now? You have had every warning.

Madeline.
[*Holding it out to him*]
Yes.

Schoen. If you offer it, I shall take it, for those are my instructions.

Madeline. Yes.

Schoen. You have no hope for recompense.

Madeline. Yes, I have.

Schoen. None whatever.
[*He takes the ring from her.*]

Madeline. The best hope I've ever had.

Schoen. What hope?

Madeline. The look in your eyes.

Schoen. I'd rather you took it back.

Madeline. No; you're to do with it as you like.

Schoen. You know what I must do with it. Yet how can I, if I remember you here, hoping that it's used for him! Take it back. You don't know what you ask of me! Suppose it's true that I'm caught in a net, that I hate it? It's evil to be in prison, but if you escape, you're an outlaw everywhere. So—one sticks to the prison, and turns the torture machine, and by and by we shall conquer the earth, no doubt, and give it a rest from torture.

Madeline. Is it true that Erfurt goes to Berlin tomorrow?

Schoen. Yes, that much was true.

Madeline. True that there's a chance of escape, that the solitary cells would let a man through?

Schoen. Yes. A little truth was mingled with the fiction. But you see, you cannot trust me, you dare not, for you will never know when my words are lies. You could never be sure that I had ceased to be your enemy.

Madeline. I'm sure of it now. I was sure of it when I called you back. And if you wished to keep your old life, if you wished to thrive as Lieutenant Schoen in Erfurt's camp—you should not have come when I called, for you knew why I called you.

Schoen. It is my duty to keep the ring.

[*He puts it in his pocket.*]
I must go.

Madeline. I shall wait for your message.

Schoen. I think there will be no message. Good night.

Madeline. Wait, let me look at you.
[*She looks into his face.*]
You see, there are tears in your eyes.

Schoen. Yes, but I have seen tears in Erfurt's eyes, when a man lay dying. And he let the man die. You must not depend on our tears.

Madeline. I shall depend on yours.

Schoen.
[*Turning away from her*]
If I call you tonight, then we shall try to work something out—we shall try to work something out together! But if I don't call, then put it all out of your mind, for there's nothing to be done!

Madeline. But you will call!

Schoen. Good night.
[*He opens the door and rushes out.*]

Madeline. Good night.
[*She stands at door a moment, then sinks to a chair.*]

CURTAIN

CANDLE IN THE WIND

ACT THREE

Madeline. They are in prison?

Deseze. They are dead. I have received the little printed slips.

Madeline. Forgive me.

Deseze. Before they come it is always possible to believe. I shall pray that as you sit here in the twilight, your hope will return to you, and that it will come true.

Madeline. Thank you.

[CHARLOTTE *and* MERCY *enter from above.* DESEZE *goes out to the right.*]

Charlotte. No, my dear, I cannot give it up, and you cannot.

Mercy. No, no. We will omit our little luxuries.—Surely we have seen this lady?

Charlotte. Yes.

Mercy. Surely we have seen you here, many times?

Madeline. Yes? Yes, I remember.

Mercy. Only you hardly knew us at first, because we are changed.

Madeline. A little, perhaps.

Charlotte. No, a great deal. In our faces. I know I see it in my sister's face. Something shining and secret.

Madeline. You have had good fortune?

Charlotte. Wonderful fortune.

Mercy. Shall we tell her our secret?

Charlotte. I think so. Yes. You see, we had a plan for the restoration of these gardens. But nothing came of that. And something has happened to our money. It brings so little, and we are hungry.

Madeline. Yes, I know.

Mercy. Many days we walked here in these gardens. A little sad, and a little hungry. And then suddenly we saw the lake. I think I saw it first.

Charlotte. Yes, you saw it first.

Mercy. The lake was there, with the swans, and the sedge, and the water-lilies, and the path to the Orangerie. Oh, all as it was.

Charlotte. And now we no longer need help with the restoration, for we walk here in that old world daily.

Mercy. And every day as we stand at the entrance we see the lake and the old buildings, and the servants carrying fruits and sweetmeats into the Trianon. And so we have escaped these new soldiers. We're quite beyond them now. That is our secret.

Charlotte. Yes, that is our secret. Because they can't touch us here in the gardens of the past. And so we have eluded them, haven't we?

Madeline. I don't know. Perhaps we've all tried to evade them, each in his own way. I'm afraid we haven't succeeded, any of us.

[SCHOEN *enters, and walks through, looking at* MADELINE.]

Mercy. We should not have told it, Charlotte.

Charlotte. No, we should not.

Mercy. Something goes out of it. Some of the shining goes from it.

Charlotte. Yes.
> [CHARLOTTE *and* MERCY *turn to go.* SCHOEN *returns toward* MADELINE.]

Mercy. But we thank you very much.

Charlotte. Yes, we do thank you.
> [*They go out.*]

Madeline. Why am I followed here?

Schoen. I was sent to look for you.

Madeline. Yes?

Schoen. M. St. Cloud told me I would find you here.

Madeline. No, it's not true. I waited a night and a day, and another night.

Schoen. Yes, I know.

Madeline. Did you try to call me?

Schoen. No, I couldn't.

Madeline. I have nothing more to give you, and you've taught me to believe nothing.

Schoen. I've known what you would think of me, and for a time I have deserved your thoughts. But not now, for I have done what I could to help you.

Madeline. What have you done?

Schoen. I have taken the step. I have set him free. It has all gone well.

Madeline. This could be a lie!—I've schooled myself to believe nothing—I mustn't put faith in these things, or I'll go mad! And yet—you'd have nothing to gain if it were a falsehood!

Schoen. Nothing.

Madeline.
[*Going to him*]
Then where is he?

Schoen. He's here, hidden in this park.

Madeline. Here? Then why—

Schoen.
[*As she turns away, he puts a hand on her arm.*]
Please—he came this far in the night, in the prison suit. But we have found a workman who will lend him clothes, and he makes the exchange now. We planned to meet here, for he hoped you might be here.

Madeline. But he's in grave danger! They must have discovered the escape! They must have followed him!

Schoen. I made an official inspection of the empty cells this morning. He was gone, and I carefully sent the pursuit in the wrong direction. It has all gone well. You have only to wait here until he comes.

Madeline. Oh, forgive me, forgive me, for any evil I have thought of you! It was unfair to ask this of you! I knew that, and I'll never be able to thank you or to repay you! Why are you trembling?

Schoen. Is it so easy to break with all you've ever known? To thrust your neck under the axe? I have seen too many executions. But I have come to the end of this quarrel with myself. This quarrel over whether it is better to be what you are and die for it, or to be what they would have you, and live. Perhaps I have found a sort of courage.

Madeline. Where will you go?

Schoen. You must not worry about me, I have my own private war to fight. But, however it goes, not everything is lost. For I am a soldier against what I hate, and it's good to fight alone. Good-bye, and thank you.

Madeline. Good-bye Lieutenant. Whatever happens, you've brought him out of prison. God keep you, and help you through.

Schoen. God keep you both, and help you through.
    [*He goes up the steps and out to the left. Then* Deseze *enters from the lower right, and crosses to* Madeline.]

Deseze. Forgive me, mademoiselle, but a workman will pass this way, slipping through in the shadows toward the west gate.

Madeline. Deseze? Will he dare to pause a moment? We'll have time for a few words?

Deseze.
    [*Going up the steps*]
    The park is deserted in the evening, mademoiselle. Take what time you need.

Madeline. I still have his passage with me. I must give him that, and tell him how to go.

Deseze.
    [*At the top of the steps*]

We'll watch the paths both ways, Henri and I. If anyone comes we'll warn you.

[*He goes out left.* MADELINE *waits, looking off to the right. After a pause,* RAOUL *enters from the right, takes a quick look about him, and holds out his hand to* MADELINE, *who runs to him. They embrace.*]

Raoul. Dare I believe it?

Madeline. Dare I believe it? So many times I've thought I saw you, so many times I've heard a voice behind me, and turned, thinking it was yours.

Raoul. Darling, if I could hold you forever. It's been a year.

Madeline. Only a year? It's been so many years.
[*They kiss.*]
But I'm afraid you shouldn't have come here.

Raoul. No place is safe. And I had to see you. This is a miracle—a miracle like the others. If you hadn't been eternally true, if your love hadn't been stronger than all of them, I'd have been lost long ago. I don't think I can leave you again.

Madeline. Oh, but you must, if we're ever to meet again —you know you must—

Raoul. Yes, I must—but not yet. I can't go yet. Do many pass this way?

Madeline. The park's not used in the evening. We can take a few minutes.

Raoul. I have a habit of keeping in the shadows. Come.
[*He draws her back toward the hedge.*]
The Lieutenant tells me I must climb the steps and

turn right when I've passed the gate. Beyond that I know nothing. You must tell me, sweet, where do I go?

Madeline. There's only one way out of France, and that's England. I have your passage.

[*She opens her bag and takes out an envelope.*]

You can still reach Cherbourg by tomorrow evening. Yes, with a little luck I'm sure you can.

Raoul. Luck never fails me, when you remember me.

Madeline. Then it won't fail you now. You'll reach Cherbourg in time, and find the little boat, and the Captain will take you across safely; and I think there must be a God, as you said long ago, for I carried that about with me even after I'd given up!

Raoul. There must be. Because you're here—and you've somehow got me out of that hell. Your arms are real.

[*Takes her in his arms*]

I'm risen from the dead.

Madeline. And I've been dead, and I'm alive again.

[*They kiss.*]

Raoul. Forgive me.

[*He climbs the steps and looks around.*]

Just out of habit I keep looking about.

[MADELINE *follows him half-way up the steps.*]

All dark and quiet.

[*He goes down to her.*]

One thing more. Where can I go after England? I've come out of such darkness, sweet. What's happened in the world? Or is there a world? Is it all Germany now?

Madeline. No, darling. They've trampled many but they've conquered none. Even when the nations give up, the people fight them with their bare hands everywhere.

Raoul. Even here? Even here in France?

Madeline. Here and everywhere.

Raoul. Thank God, thank God, then! Oh, Madeline, I know what they're like in their horrible souls! They mean to make the whole world like the inside of that prison camp! It's desperate, this war to save the earth! As desperate as the fight you made to save me! But you and I, we're together in this now?

Madeline. In everything. They've made soldiers of us all —women and children and all. They've even made one of me. But you must go.

Raoul. Could you come with me?

Madeline. No, those who travel underground have taught me the rules: Travel fast, travel light, and travel alone. But don't worry about me—I know all the ways there are, and I'm in no danger.

Raoul. When will I see you?

Madeline. There are three pencilled words on the outside of the envelope I gave you. Go first where they direct you. From there they'll know. Oh, Raoul, do lovers never have long years together?

Raoul. It used to happen. It will happen again.

Madeline. For other lovers. Lovers to come!

Raoul. No, dear, for us!

Madeline. Keep safe.

Raoul. Keep safe, darling.
> [*He kisses her, then goes up the steps.*]

You must not be seen with me. Perhaps you should wait here a moment, then leave by the other gate.

Madeline. Yes, darling. Till England!

Raoul. Till England!
> [*He goes out to the left. She runs up the steps, looking after him.* HENRI *enters downstage right.*]

Henri. Mademoiselle?

Madeline. Yes. Yes, Henri.

Henri. He's gone?

Madeline. Yes, he's gone.

Henri. I burned the prison clothes. There's no trace left.

Madeline. He should be through the gates by now.
> [*She comes down to him.*]

Will you look, Henri? I don't dare.
> [HENRI *climbs the steps and meets* DESEZE, *entering.*]

Deseze. He's gone.

Madeline. Yes?

Deseze. He will be safe. He went through the gates, and I closed them after him. There was nobody east or west. It's early to close the gates, but it seemed better if they were shut. He turned east along the road under the trees. I think he will be safe!

Madeline. Thank you. It was impossible, and it's happened!

[*She starts to cry, takes a handkerchief out of her bag, and wipes her eyes.*]

I thought I had no tears left, but for happiness I have. You've put yourselves in danger, both of you.

Henri. He's a soldier of France, mademoiselle.

Madeline. There are no two people in all France I shall hate so much to leave.

Deseze. You will leave us, mademoiselle?

Madeline. I want to be in London when he comes. And somehow I will, somehow I will. Once when he came safely out of the sea, he said that my hand had been over him there on the water. Now I know what he meant—for his hand is over me now. Good-bye, Henri.—

[*She starts up the steps. A whistle blows in the distance.*]

What does that mean?

Henri. I've never heard it here before. I don't know.

[*He goes up to the top of the steps.*]

There are soldiers entering the park.

Deseze. It's dangerous for you to stay here, mademoiselle. I have the key to the other gate. I'll let you through that way.

[*He starts up the steps.*]

Madeline.

[*Following him up*]

Yes, please, if you will.

[*She stops.*]

No, I'll stay here.

Henri. Please, mademoiselle.

Deseze. They won't see you, if you come quickly.

Madeline. No, you go, Deseze, and you, Henri. I'll stay here. The longer they spend with me, the further he'll be on his way.

Deseze. Then we'll stay, too. They'll find nothing against us, mademoiselle.

Madeline. You're sure you're safe?

Henri. There's nothing left, not a footprint.
   [*They all stand waiting. Off stage to the right a German* OFFICER *is heard giving orders. Another replies. Then a whistle blows nearby.* CORPORAL SCHULTZ *enters.*]

Schultz. It will be necessary for you to remain here. All of you. You too, Fraeulein, wait here.

Madeline. How long must we wait?

Schultz. You must wait here to be questioned.

Madeline.
   [*Crossing to him*]
   Can you tell me why we are being detained, Corporal?

Schultz. I believe there has been an escape from the prison camp and the pursuit comes this way. But do not be alarmed, Fraeulein. We seek only the fugitives.
   [*A German* CAPTAIN *enters above, followed by* GUARDS.]

Captain. Fuehren Sie sie herueber.
   [*Some* GUARDS *cross the stage, some take positions on the steps, one examines the papers of those detained.*]

Papiere von allen Personen untersuchen. Vorwaerts!

Guard. Zu Befehl, Herr Hauptmann.
   [*He goes down the steps.*]

Captain.
> [*To* MADELINE]

We are bringing together all the people in the park.

Guard. Your papers.
> [HENRI *and* DESEZE *show their cards.*]

May I see your papers, please?
> [MADELINE *shows her passport.*]
> [A GUARD *re-enters from left.*]

Guard. Kein Mensch im Park.

Captain. Niemand im Park?

Guard. Wir haben alles abgesucht. Es ist mir einfach ein Raetsel, wo der Kerl hingekommen ist.
> [*Two more* GUARDS *enter and are directed by the* CAPTAIN *to take positions on the steps.*]

Captain. Ist alles fertig für Herrn Oberst?

Corporal. Jawohl. Wir haben drei Personen hier.

Captain. Gut gemacht.
> [ERFURT *enters from the upper right.*]

Erfurt. Hat jemand den Park verlassen?

Captain. Wir haben niemand gesehen.

Erfurt. Wo ist St. Cloud?

Captain. St. Cloud ist nicht im Park.

Erfurt. Warum warten Sie noch? Good evening, Miss Guest.
> [*He goes down two steps, sees* HENRI *and* DESEZE.]

Wer sind die? Haben die ihre Ausweispapiere?

Corporal. Jawohl, Herr Oberst.

Erfurt. Verhoeren Sie sie.

Guard. Come with me.
[HENRI *and* DESEZE *are led out.*]

Erfurt. Wer sind die zwei?

Captain. Parkaufseher.

Erfurt. Vielleicht können Sie aus denen etwas heraus bekommen?

Captain. Jawohl, Herr Oberst.

Erfurt.
[*Going down steps*]
Miss Guest?

Madeline. Yes, Colonel Erfurt?

Erfurt. We looked for you at your hotel, but you were gone. When I returned from Berlin this morning, there had been an escape at the camp. Lieutenant Schoen was connected with it. He has disappeared, and we have traced him to Versailles, and to these gardens. You haven't seen him today, by chance?

Madeline. No.

Erfurt. Now it may be I have lost Schoen, but you, my dear Miss Guest, could be quite as useful. Wachen abtreten.

Captain. Wachen abtreten.
[*The* CAPTAIN *and the* GUARDS *go out.*]

Erfurt. Where is Raoul St. Cloud?

Madeline. I don't know.

Erfurt. You do know, of course. You told me once that you would do this. Now, by a combination of chances, you have succeeded. Where is he?

Madeline. Suppose I did tell you—how would you know I hadn't lied to you?

Erfurt. Of course, it will be necessary to hold you until your lover has been recaptured.

Madeline. You wouldn't dare!

Erfurt. Yes, I would dare. You are guilty of a major crime. Your name will not protect you.

Madeline. I was not thinking of my name, but of my nation.

Erfurt. If you had been a French woman, you would have been arrested, and your money confiscated, a year ago. We let you alone because of your nationality, and your name. But we no longer care greatly what you think of us. You will help me to recapture this prisoner or you will face trial for aiding in his escape.

Madeline. You could let me go. I am only to meet him— sometime—a long way from here—if I can find him. There's so little chance of any happiness. You could let me go.

Erfurt. Only if I have him in your place. Ask anything you like for St. Cloud, except his freedom, and you shall have it. I'll make his captivity light. I'll save his life if I can. You shall see him as often as you like—but his freedom he must not have.

Madeline. But he is free.

Erfurt. Very doubtfully. We'll catch up with him, wherever he is.

Madeline. If you're so certain of that, why do you ask my help? I think you've lost him, and you think so too. As for your promises to treat him well, no child would believe you.

Erfurt. No? As yet you have not understood me. I must have him or I must give an accounting to Berlin. I don't think I could find the words to say to my superiors: St. Cloud is free. They might be my last words, my last in office, my last as what I am.

Madeline. But you will say them.

Erfurt. No. I cannot say them. I shall have to employ whatever means I have to make you speak.

Madeline. And you believe you could make me speak?

Erfurt. There is no human will—not even a fanatic's, not even a lover's—that can hold out against us.

Madeline. I have been told that the lovers are a great trouble to your tribunals. That the beaters are inclined to throw down their whips when a woman in love is brought before them.

Erfurt. Yes? Where did you hear this?

Madeline. I've made a study of you this year past.

Erfurt. I've spoken very gently, because my power is absolute. My fear is that I must use it. I beg of you, do not make me use it.

Madeline. Your power is not absolute, Colonel Erfurt, because you must answer to your government for what you do! And your government is not absolute because it must answer to the world! You will not hold me, and your government will not hold me! You dare not add to your enemies, for already you are surrounded by enemies. A cold wind of hatred blows at you from every corner of the earth! You have felt that wind before, and you know what it means. It means that you will lose. You wear these gorgeous uniforms and stage yourself so elaborately and talk in such loud voices to cover your emptiness and your fear!

Erfurt. There is no need to discuss your civilization or mine! We are hard here because we must be, and your case is like another and must be dealt with!

Madeline. Very well! He's free. Raoul is free! Do as you like with me! Take your revenge! But you must still go to Berlin and tell them Raoul is free!

Erfurt. Hauptman!

[*The* CAPTAIN *enters with three* GUARDS.]

Take a last look about you at your free world! I have not yet spoken tho word that will shut you up, but when I do speak it I will not take it back!

Madeline.

[*Looking at the* GUARDS, *then at* ERFURT]

I came into this fight tardily and by chance, and unwilling. I never thought to die young, or for a cause. But now that I've seen you close, now that I know you, I'd give my life gladly to gain one half inch against you! And I'll never again be worth so much against you as I am now, if you arrest me here this evening. If you think you have anything to gain by it, arrest me, imprison me, put a final end to me! It will be known! And it will not be easy to explain! Berlin will not thank you!

[*There is a pause.*]

Lash out and give the order if you're not afraid!
[*There is no answer. She turns and goes up to the top of the steps.*]

Erfurt. It is true that it is not expedient to arrest you now. But give me your passport. You are now a prisoner in France.
[*She gives him her passport.*]

We take our enemies one at a time, and your country is last on the list. But your time will come.

Madeline. Yes. We shall expect you and be ready for you. In the history of the world, there have been many wars between men and beasts. And the beasts have always lost, and men have won.
[*She goes out.*]

CURTAIN